# Train Up Your Children in the Way They Should Eat

## A Healthy Child Instruction Manual

### By SHARON BROER
with Dr. Ted Broer

Health Masters 100 Ariana Blvd, Auburndale, FL 33823

B & A Publications

1-800-726-1834    1-800-592-4325
www.healthmasters.com

1

Train Up Your Children in the Way They Should Eat
by Sharon Broer
Published by B & A Publications
100 Ariana Blvd.
Auburndale, Florida 33823

Unless otherwise noted, all Scripture quotations are from the King James Version of the Bible.

Scripture quotations marked NIV are from the Holy Bible, New International Version, Copyright 1973, 1978, 1984, International Bible Society, Used by permission.

Scripture notations marked NLT are from the Holy Bible. New Living Translation, copyright 1996. Used by permission of Tyndale House Publishers, Inc., Wheaton, IL 60189. All rights reserved.

*A note about the sidebars in this book:* I have drawn from many sources and authorities to provide interesting and informative sidebars. I don't always agree with the overall philosophy of the sources, but when helpful statements come from books or articles, we can benefit from them nevertheless. You can find the sources for the sidebars with endnote numbers in the Notes section. "Adapted" means that I have changed the wording somewhat or condensed the information to fit into a reasonable space; naturally, I have still credited the source. Otherwise, the material is a direct quote. If there is not an endnote number with a sidebar, that material comes from me.

---SHARON BROER

In order to protect the privacy of people involved in Sharon's workshops, names and places have been changed.

Most of us hope and pray we choose wisely when finding that perfect mate to share our life. I thank God I chose wisely, and I want to dedicate this manual to my incredible husband, Ted, who has been so supportive in everything I've chosen to do. At times it seems he has believed in me more than I believed in myself. Along with my relationship with the Lord, he has helped make my life a continuous adventure in learning and enjoyment. He is my best friend and business partner, and words could never express my love, appreciation and admiration for him.

Ted, thank you for helping make our journey fun, exciting and something to look forward to every single day. You're my hero!

# CONTENTS

# PART III:

## THE PROCESS: A CHANGE OF HEART AND HABITS

5

# <u>FOREWARD</u>

## *Train Up Your Children In the Way They Should Eat*

During the past twenty-five years it has been my pleasure to have my wife, Sharon, on my team in helping to instruct millions of individuals globally on the merits of proper nutrition and lifestyle choices. During this time we have both developed a deep-seated passion for children. Our passion does not only encompass the many and varied aspects of raising physically healthy children. We are also passionate in our desire to see children trained in how to function as champions in an ever-changing world. By pursuing this passion together, we feel that we have learned how to raise mentally, physically and spiritually balanced children who excel in all that they do.

My wife rode horses for twelve years, and she competed on a national level. Often she has told me how important it was to train her animals properly. The training and care of her horses not only entailed thousands of hours of practice, but proper nutritional and rest patterns as well. She would never have taken an expensive horse, kept it out all hours of the night, fed it Twinkies and Ding Dongs, along with sodas, and expected the animal to perform well, much less stay healthy. In fact, she even makes sure that if a stray cat or a neighbor's dog comes by, she has a good quality food available for it. My son Austin has a five-dollar guinea pig that gets the remnants of our organic apples and greens. Most of you take very good care of your pets and would never feed them junk food.

This, however, brings me to a very strange question. Why is it so many people take better care of their pets, from a nutritional standpoint, than they do their children? Why is it that the leading cause of death in our children, next to accidents, is cancer? Why are

6

so many of our children plagued with asthma, obesity, allergies, attention deficit hyperactivity disorder and other types of learning disabilities? Could it be that the junk we are feeding them is playing a vital role in the demise of their health?

This book addresses these issues and much, much more. If gives you, the reader, an opportunity for introspection to help you ask yourself, "Is there some way to provide healthier food choices for my family?" Remember, as an adult, your health is your responsibility! It's not your doctor's, your spouses or your next-door neighbor's; it's *your* responsibility. But remember that your child's health is your responsibility too. Our children don't drive to the store and bring back junk; we parents do.

If you are overweight, you already know the embarrassment, pain and rejection this can cause. So many parents who are overweight have children who are following in their footsteps. Many blame their children for being obese, or they blame genetics, the school, the day care or their neighbors. But I've got another question for you. Why is it that a lot of overweight people have overweight pets? There is obviously no genetic link.

President Harry Truman had a plaque on his desk that said, "The buck stops here!" When it comes to the nutrition of your children, the buck stops with you! Please read this manual and start making healthier choices for you and your family's nutritional needs. I promise you that the rewards of having a healthy, physically fit, mentally alert and top-performing child is well worth the effort. Remember, our children and their health are precious gifts from God, so please treat your gift accordingly.

DR. Ted Broer

# PREFACE

When I married Ted, I thought I was enjoying pretty good health. As Ted started working with me, though, we discovered that my health was far from good.

Changing my diet made all the difference.

The next step was to ask myself, *how do I cook and prepare foods that are healthy for my entire family?* I knew this line of thinking would lead to a book one day—and here it is. It covers the issues I've been researching and teaching in workshops for several years. It's been developed over a period of time that has included having a miscarriage, finally becoming pregnant with my son Austin and now raising my son Harrison and daughters Alexis and Savannah. I hope you'll find the chapters informative and practical. I also hope you'll be inspired to eat healthy and teach your children to do so as well.

I thank God for bringing Ted and me together and for allowing us to spread the message of healthy eating and living. I pray that this book will help you and your family make the dietary changes necessary for an abundant life. It's not only possible, but it's also quite fun!

# INTRODUCTION

## *Why I'm Passionate About Your Children's Health*

I was raised back in the 60's and 70's, the days when junk food was just beginning to be a staple of the American diet. In fact, as far back as I can remember, I was munching salted pork rinds, frosted snack cakes and aluminum-wrapped TV dinners. My breakfasts consisted of Life cereal and Pop-Tarts (with the chocolate icing), all washed down with Instant Breakfast drink mix—chocolate, of course. I must have made a few junk food companies a pretty hefty profit.

Bless my mother's heart, it's not her fault. Just like the rest of the moms in those days, she reveled in the convenience of picking up those new packaged foods. Think of the time saved! I mean, lets have a reality check here. How many of our parents ever took a single class in nutrition? They were raised before the onslaught of junk food and thousands of chemical food additives; they knew nothing about the dangers of such products.

No, it's not that my parents didn't love me with all their hearts; they just weren't educated in nutrition. The whole topic wasn't very popular. After all, the people in those days who ate healthy—or "weird"—were the hippies, right? They might talk about organics or health food co-ops, but they also had some pretty bad habits of their own. In fact, it's because of the stereotypic health food hippie weirdos that the health food movement has had such a difficult time being accepted. So, I don't blame any of my health problems on my parents. It just wasn't the norm to eat healthy.

### *Early Anchors:  Sweet, Fat and Caffeinated*

We all grew up on what I call our childhood "anchor foods"— favorite foods from our past, certain foods that bring back happy childhood memories. What were they for you?

I grew up in the South, so the first thing that comes to mind is homemade banana pudding. You know the kind: made with ripe, sliced bananas and vanilla wafers, topped off with fluffy, oven-baked meringue. Not that it was such a bad food, but it certainly proved no hindrance to my fast-developing sweet tooth. Another fondly remembered anchor food was a family favorite:  tacos made with ground beef and refried beans. The pork lard (which is incredibly bad for you) in the beans made them taste so good.

My father was an officer in the Air Force, so we lived overseas quite a bit, spending about three years in England. That's where I learned to

9

love still another of my anchor foods: tea.   I was old enough to walk by then, so if my mother couldn't find me at 11:00 a.m. in the morning or 4:00 p.m. in the afternoon, I was next door at our neighbor's having a "spot of tea" and biscuits.  I'm quite sure the English weren't serving "unleaded" tea back then, so I was hooked on caffeine at a very young age.

From England, we moved to France, where I remember riding on the little passenger seat of my mother's bike to a town where we got our bread.  I grew up on the nice, two-foot-long French bread in the narrow white paper bag.  It wasn't exactly Wonder Bread, but it got me started on white, processed flour just the same.

My father was eventually stationed at Eglin Air Force Base on Florida's northern gulf coast.  There we'd go to The Wharf, a little restaurant featuring fried cube steak and fried shrimp.  At least once a week we'd order carry out, bring those greasy-smelling, moist brown bags back to the kitchen table and then dig into deep-fat fried shrimp and deep-fat fried steak.  As bad as it was for my arteries, I can still remember the aroma even now.

Of course, my mom cooked a lot of fried foods at home, too.  You may remember the days of the little can of bacon grease that our mothers always kept on the stove.  That's what most of my food was cooked in.  It was the Southern way.  I ate lots of French fries cooked in bacon grease, lots of pork chops and a few collard greens or black-eyed peas flavored by the contents of that little can.

As soon as I learned to drive at sixteen, my parents would give me $100, and I'd go down to the base commissary to buy a whole month's worth of family groceries.  (Yes, back in the 1970's, $100 could still buy a month of groceries.)  Mom would give me a strict shopping list, but she allowed me to get certain "extras" for myself.  (Actually, I had free reign.)  After I bought the beef, Hamburger Helper and all the basic things that anchored our diet, I headed for the frozen TV dinners, the Doritos and the Little Debbie snack cakes.  I think I tried every variety of Little Debbie snack cakes made at the time.  (My favorites were the chocolate ones with white swirls inside.  But I also loved the oatmeal ones, with all that white, gooey "stuffing" in the middle.)

Then, of course, I'd buy several boxes of Moon Pies. (You're probably starting to think this sounds like a pretty good diet! In reality, however, it might have sustained life, but it didn't allow for good health. Read on to learn the rest of the story!)

And boy, could I eat! I was riding horses quite a bit as a kid, competing in shows and hanging around the stable most of the day. I played and worked hard, and due to my genetics and metabolism, I was pretty skinny. I remember that after most of the horse shows, my mom would make me those tacos with the pork-larded beans, and I could sit down and eat four or five instantly. I was thin, but thin doesn't mean healthy. Certainly it didn't mean I was eating right.

You see, if it was sweet, if it was fat, if it was caffeinated...it was for me!

## *"You've Definitely Got a Problem"*

Even with all the junk and all the bad food habits I'd indulged in growing up, it seemed to have little effect on my health. I was rarely sick, never developed food allergies, and never went to the hospital—all due to my good constitution. I'd been the picture of health as far as I and my parents were concerned. It wasn't until I left home and went to college that it all caught up with me.

I was working in retail, and I also held a stressful part-time modeling job while taking a full load at Florida State University. I had no extra time—running from classes, to first job, to second job, to library, until all hours of the night. Each morning it started over again. Naturally, I ate on the run—I ate junk.

We're talking mint chocolate chip ice cream for breakfast. If anyone could have been called a "junkaholic", I was president of the club. I remember going to the fast food drive through and just inhaling fries and milkshakes. I stayed in the car because I was eating by the clock; I had to get it all down before walking in for my next job. Amazingly, my body allowed me to do this for a solid year.

I'd moved into an apartment with my dear friend Wanda, the most wonderful roommate I ever had, and she was the one who witnessed my body's ignoble fall from junk food glory.

We were sound asleep…until I woke up screaming.

*I can hardly breathe,* I thought. *And this pain is going to kill me, for sure!* I started to panic. I couldn't talk, the shooting pains in my abdomen cutting through me like a knife. Wanda heard me moaning and ran into the room.

"Sharon, what is wrong with you?"

"Wanda, I don't know what's wrong with me! It's my stomach—I feel as if I have a knife in my stomach!" I was crying and screaming in agony.

"Do I call an ambulance?"

I knew my mom was visiting her mother in Tallahassee at that time, so I blurted, "No, call my mother! Have her meet us at the hospital."

I could barely move, could hardly get into the car and couldn't get out of the car once we arrived at the hospital. The nurses came out and carried me into a room. There a middle-aged doctor immediately said, "so, what in the world did you do to yourself?"

I honestly couldn't think of what I had done. Surely nothing wrong. Everything had been going along in routine fashion: the jobs, the classes, and the fast food drive-thru.

"Well, Doctor," I managed to mumble, "last night, I ate at a fast food Mexican restaurant. But that's never bothered me before."

The doctor ran several tests and then came back shaking his head. "Sharon, we can't find anything wrong."

So he ran more tests. Finally, after what seemed like hours, he came back into the room and said, "You've definitely got a problem, young lady—but an unusual one."

*Great!* I thought. *Is this going to take me off my schedule?*

"You don't have an ulcer," he said, "but you do have an irritated gut."

An irritated gut? It didn't sound very "medical" to me.

"Well, you might call it an aggravated stomach. What's happened is that your diet and your lifestyle have caused your stomach to swell up like a balloon. Every time you breathe, your lungs rub up against the top of your stomach wall, and it feels like sandpaper." He told me I was staying in the hospital overnight. "And then, for the next two months you're going to eat only bland foods," he said. "You're going to drink only milk or water. Eventually, that mistreated stomach of yours should calm back down."

I'd never been so sick. The nutritional light bulb, however, was starting to turn on.

### *"Sharon, You Don't Have a Choice"*

My mother nursed me back to a semblance of health on mashed potatoes and Jell-O. Then I quit one of my jobs because I knew I had thoroughly overextended myself and was totally stressed out. Finally, I graduated.

Once out of college, I began to think, *Looks like I'm completely healthy again.* My diet didn't change—I still had ice cream for breakfast. I still ate lunch on the run. I remember getting that packaged ham luncheon meat, the kind that when you peel off the plastic lid, it has an orangey-yellow metallic color to it (I didn't know it was the nitrates). I would cut the meat in little thin slices and roll them up with cream cheese. I thought that was healthy. Little did I know.

You see, I'd always believed that if I didn't have a major disease such as cancer, diabetes or heart disease, I was healthy. Have you felt that way too? Many of us assume that if we "only" have indigestion, headaches, heartburn, nervousness, fatigue, allergies, constipation, depression, menstrual problems...then we're perfectly fine. Yet one way to determine the true state of our health is to take an objective look inside our medicine cabinets. The average American's medicine chest contains large doses of antacids, painkillers, cough medicines, decongestants, tranquilizers, aspirins, antidepressants and much more. But think about this: Do people have headaches because they have an aspirin deficiency? Do people take Rolaids because they have an antacid deficiency? No! I hadn't realized that my constant headaches were caused by my body's elevated blood sugars. I would fight the symptoms of those headaches on a daily basis, but I had little idea how to fight the cause of the pain. I intended to find out, though.

I attended a nutrition conference in Tallahassee, and Ted Broer was one of the speakers. Several months later I was introduced to Ted, and three years later we started dating. On our first date Ted asked me if it would be OK if we went out for dinner. He took me to a Shoney's restaurant and asked me, "What would you like?" I said, "I want a hot fudge cake." So I ate a hot fudge cake. He said, "Would you like another one?" I replied, "Yes I would!" (Needless to say, I don't recommend this approach on a first date—or any date for that matter.) So I had two hot fudge cakes on our first date. (Don't do this, girls!) Ted knew there had to be a problem because I was very thin, and I had just displayed an incredible capacity for...well...hot fudge cakes.

Except for my infamous "Night of the Killer Cramps," I'd still never really been sick. I was apparently the picture of health. I think the modeling made me clamp down on eating for certain periods so I could binge at other times. It kept me from developing a weight problem, but it also kept my system thoroughly out of balance.

Several days after those two monster desserts, Ted proposed to me over a Wendy's grilled chicken sandwich at Silver Lake in Tallahassee. About that same time he decided to start a nutrition counseling practice in Winter Haven, Florida. I decided that I wanted to go with him.

Within a few months we were married, and we moved into our new life together.

During that first year, Ted was getting over a heart disease. He had counseling appointments throughout the day at his office, but he'd have to take a break in the middle of every day to take a three-hour nap because he'd been so sick. Here he was taking naps, and here I am, Little Miss Sugarholic still gorging myself with chocolate and junk food—so hyper I'm jumping off the walls! *What is wrong with him? Look at me—I have all this energy! Why doesn't he have it too?* Ted would eventually get back to health and great energy, but I had no idea that my so-called "energy" was mostly an adrenalin and sugar high. I was overtaxing my adrenal glands and making myself sicker and sicker as the days went by.

After we were married for a while, I did tell Ted that I suffered headaches in my temples every day. I'd been eating three to four chocolate bars a day. I got a sugar high and would go work out in the gym and be buzzing. An hour later, I'd have such a headache I could barely take the pain. I didn't know what was happening. Struggling with his own health recovery, Ted seemed even more worried about me. He'd done a lot of work with blood sugar levels, hypoglycemia and diabetes, so he did a test in his office to check my sugar levels. He came in after he did the test and said, "Sharon, you don't have a choice. Something has to change. Your sugar levels are off the charts. They're so high you could be prescribed insulin immediately."

### *I Thought, Needles?*

He got my attention. That's the day that turned my health around.

"There are two ways we can attempt to do this," Ted said. "You can go cold turkey, weather the withdrawal symptoms and just stop all sugar and chocolate overnight. Or, we can start on your insulin shots."

I didn't want plan B. I hate needles!

"No, I want to go cold turkey and get off this stuff,"

No more candy bars, no more ice cream. In effect, no more shiny, gooey, sticky, creamy "stuff" posing as food.

That headache in my temples had started to leave me though. After eating so much sugar and not drinking any water, my body had never had the chance to cleanse itself and get the sugar levels down. I'd been overloading my pancreas, and my blood sugar levels stayed at a constant high. Ted put me on steam-distilled water, and the cleansing process began.

A few days later, Ted raised another topic: "I guess we'll have to change the way we cook around here, too, honey." He really didn't want to say this to me when we first got married. Remember all that good Southern cooking I'd learned to love? It's hard for anyone to meddle with his spouse's happiness. But now it was time to be making some changes. Ted could see that we had a major problem. If I didn't make major changes, he would have to deal with a very sick wife.

The wonderful thing is that our bodies are so merciful to us that they will take a lot. We, however, treat them unmercifully, filling them with so much that robs them of energy and flirts with harm. As strong as they are, our bodies are going to start breaking down eventually if we don't make some changes. It happened with me a little sooner than later. But that precious package of blood and bone and muscle—which we think we love so much—can only take so much abuse. But here's the good news: I listened to Ted and changed my diet, my sugar levels returned to normal and my health improved dramatically. More on this later!

### *Today, Children Are Still in Trouble!*

Now that you know my story, can you see why I'm so passionate about children's nutrition? It's because of what happened to my own health and my ongoing memories about the lingering results of my childhood filled with sweets and fats. I had been so unhealthy for so many years that when I finally had my son Austin and started nursing him, he took every little bit of energy I had left in my body. I was so weak that I could barely walk up the stairs. My blood pressure dropped to 60 over 40. I had been so unhealthy for so many years before my pregnancy, and my body gave every ounce of nutrition it had left to make a healthy child. Our son is healthy, but it depleted me. If I had to do it over again, I'd have prepared myself with better nutrition in the earlier years. What pains me to the core, though, is knowing that my story is hardly unique. No doubt you noticed several points of contact with your own nutritional history as you read this introduction. At the beginning, I spoke of the 60's and 70's as an era of junk foods. But we all know that, if anything, it's much worse today. That's why I harbor a deep passion for the children of today and the children of the decades to come.

Our children are gifts from God. They are so precious, so innocent, so inquisitive, so full of life. Yet they are dying. Fifty, or even thirty years ago, we were shocked to hear the terrible news of a child stricken with cancer. Today, the leading cause of death in children under the age of fourteen, other than accidents, is cancer. When you hear that horrible statistic, does it cut into your heart as it does mine? In fact, my heart was deeply touched recently while I sat in church looking over the bulletin before the service started. Each week, in the middle of the bulletin there's a one-page list of members or friends asking for prayer. As I scanned through the names, I began counting how many of those prayer requests were for children: children who had been stricken with stomach cancer, leukemia, brain tumor, lymphatic cancer…the list went on. I started thinking about how the parents of those children must feel and the pain they must be enduring for their beloved offspring.

The only way we are going to see any change in the health of our children is to take charge, become educated in nutrition and move into action. In other words, we parents and grandparents need to wake up. The children of today don't have to be so sick. Wonderful, healthy changes can be made, but they have to start at home. Your child's health is not your child's responsibility, not your doctor's responsibility, not their teacher's responsibility. It is *your* responsibility. You are totally responsible for your child's health.

How thankful Ted and I are for having healthy children. These days I'm raising our second little boy, Harrison, and our two daughters, Alexis and Savannah. Harrison has been helping me write this book for you, because everything I'm asking you to do with your little ones, I've been doing with him and his sisters. As I look into his eyes, I see his complete trust in my love and protection. My eyes echo back the desire of my heart to provide everything he needs. I sense too the heartbeat of mothers across this land who want the very best for their own children.

Train up a child in the way he should go: and when he
is old, he will not depart from it.

Proverbs 22:6

Remember, knowledge is power. Let us do as this ancient proverb calls us to do. We can train our children for a better life. We can give them the experience and knowledge they need to thrive and grow strong. Such training will form habits and patterns in them that will last a lifetime—hopefully, a very long lifetime. I firmly believe our children can avoid the past mistakes we may have made with our own nutrition. They just need to be trained. We parents are here to train them.

# PART I:

## THE PROBLEM:
## A GENERATION AT RISK

# 1

\*\*\*\*\*\*\*

# *What's Happening to Our Children's Health?*

$M$Y FRIEND RITA is the most loving and giving parent I know. But her story still breaks my heart. I'll let her tell it in her own words....

### *Child in Crisis: A Case Study*

"Rita, this is the healthiest baby I've ever seen."

That was the hospital pediatrician talking as he smiled down at my pudgy newborn, Daniel. It made me feel so good to hear those words. My husband, Bill, and I had tried to do everything right during the pregnancy to make sure we'd have a healthy baby.

Our first little boy, and he's so beautiful!

When Daniel was two weeks old, I took him to the doctor's office for the typical two-week-baby check-up. He'd been born in the wintertime, so when we were ushered into a waiting room, we sat down among a roomful of sick children, all coughing and sniffling with the flu. As our wait began, I held Daniel close, occasionally asking for an individual room. But the nurse said, "Sorry, its crazy today; we're booked."

And the waiting went on…one hour…two hours…

Within twenty-four hours of arriving back home, Daniel and I both came down with the flu. Our two-week-old little boy was very sick.

I called the doctor.

"Go to the drug store," he said. "Put him on one of the over-the-counter flu medicines for his age group. The little tyke should be fine in a couple days."

But after a full six weeks of flu-like symptoms, we couldn't get him well; he continued to get sicker and sicker. I was told to take him off breast milk.

I'd been nursing Daniel, and I thought, *At least this is one thing that's helping!* But I took him off the breast for about forty-eight hours. Then, seeing no changes, I put him back on and refused to take him off the breast thereafter. (Of course, now I know, after more in-depth study on nutrition, that breast-feeding Daniel was one of the best things I could have done for him.) The problem was that I still had a very sick baby.

For six more weeks Daniel and I couldn't go outside. I couldn't take those long-imagined strolls in the park with my new baby, pushing the little blue carriage we'd gotten for him. We couldn't sit out on a blanket in the spring sunshine and watch the clouds and butterflies. Little Daniel was awfully sick, confined to his crib. And my husband and I were truly worried.

### *"It's Standard Procedure"*

By the time Daniel was a year old, he was in the hospital with sores in his mouth. He hadn't been genuinely healthy since his first two weeks of life. "We're working on it," said our new doctor. "We really want to get to the bottom on this too." Daniel had uncontrollable chronic diarrhea and bleeding rashes on his buttocks. Before he'd gone into the hospital, we did everything from changing to three different types of diapers, to using any kind of antibiotic and over-the-counter drugs the doctor could pump down him. We kept our regular weekly visits to the pediatrician's office with one goal in mind: Please, please, make him well!

Most of the time, Daniel could eat or drink very little. He was dehydrating. He stayed in the hospital for five days while nurses gave him Kool-Aid, diluted soda pop, Jell-O and many other things filled with sugar and food colorings. "It's standard procedure," said the doctors. "Look, he's holding these things down. That's good news."

I didn't know any better. We'd made up our minds to work with those doctors and to follow every suggestion and prescription to the letter. Nothing was more important to us than getting our poor little baby back to health. I wanted to see those blue eyes smile at me once again. The doctors did everything they could, but still no progress. At the end of the five-day hospitalization, I'd had all I could take. I went into my bedroom and stayed up all night…pacing, weeping, and praying.

"Look Rita," Bill said. "Maybe the little guy just wasn't born strong enough. Maybe his body doesn't have what it takes to

22

fight these things. He might be kind of sickly all his life." But I knew he'd been the picture of health at birth. I remembered the beaming pediatrician as I held Daniel's fat little body. His ribs weren't showing through then, and his skin was so rosy pink. I was going to have a child like that again. I knew something was terribly wrong; I just didn't know what it was.

Two weeks later Daniel was back in the hospital. He had all the other former symptoms, but now he was also pulling at his ears. "Doctor," I said, "if we even touch his ears, he screams in pain. And he runs high fevers night after night." So it went, another round of prescriptions, another round of doctor visits and specialists, more anxious nights and worrisome days. And it all went on for a solid year and a half.

### *"There Has to Be Another Way"*

By the time our son was two years old, we'd taken him to several ear, nose and throat specialists. The latest doctor checked his ears and ran him through hundreds of dollars' worth of allergy tests. "It appears Daniel is going to need ear surgery," he told us. "First, take this serum home with you, along with these needles, and give Daniel allergy shots every day. We'll show you how to do it." I was stunned. Weeks of giving Daniel painful shots, more weeks of suffering with ear pain and fever, all to culminate in cutting him with a scalpel? "You see, he's rapidly losing his hearing. He has fluid and infection in his ears. Surgery is your best bet," the doctor told us. The thought of surgery did give me some hope. *Maybe this is the cure after all.* I was panicked, but I was willing to try anything if it would only relieve this little child's suffering.

Then, a couple of weeks before the operation, the doctors showed me a film on the risks that come with the ear surgery we were supposed to book for Daniel. One of the three major risks was total hearing loss.  I thought, ***God that just doesn't seem like the answer to me.***

I went to choir practice at my church the next night, thoroughly discouraged, and asked some of the ladies to stay after practice to pray with me.  We'd already booked the surgery for Daniel, but I thought there had to be another way.  That's when one of the ladies told me about the Broer's and their work with nutrition and health.  She said, "They've done their homework, Rita.  I really believe they can help you."

I called them the very next morning, and Bill and I went to their office right away.  They ran some screening tests on Daniel, and I was so impressed that I let them give me a screening too.  They told us, "We think we know what's wrong with your little boy. If you'll do what we tell you, in thirty days you'll have a different child."

I'm going to save the ending to Rita's story for the conclusion of this chapter.  (Sure, you can peek, if you like!)  But for now, let's consider some of the things that can go wrong with a child's health simply because of the way he's eating.

## *Junior's Diet…and His Health Problems*

Rita's story is more common than you think.  Not all children will suffer for the length of time that Daniel did, but many do suffer. When we bring home a healthy baby from the hospital, we naturally expect that baby to continue to grow and thrive. When it doesn't happen, the picture is just wrong.

## *Not a Picture of Health*

My point in telling Rita's story is simply to drive home the central theme of this entire book.  I want to make it as real and urgent as possible: Your child's health is solidly tied to what he

24

eats. I could write volumes on the kinds of health problems that stem from poor nutrition, obesity, and cholesterol and chemical additive ingestion. But in this chapter I'll just highlight the basics you need to know in order to start making changes for the better. If this quick review awakens you to the danger of being lackadaisical about your child's nutrition, then I will have accomplished a worthy goal. Now for those diet-related health problems…

### *Ear Infections*

I'm still amazed at the number of mothers and grandmothers who tell me their baby or grandchild is constantly having ear infections and is constantly on antibiotics. My first response is, "Is your baby on formula?" Invariably, the answer is, "Of course!" (In chapter five we'll go into depth about the hazards of today's baby formulas, and I'll show you how to make your own for a healthier child.)

Just last month, a mother came up to me in a park playground and proceeded to explain how her little nine-month old girl had suffered ear infections since the day they'd adopted her at six months. She was starting her fourth month of antibiotics. I asked this worried mom if she'd like to try some simple dietary changes that might help her little girl. She was eager to take whatever action she needed to take.

First, she took her baby off store-bought formula and found a goat farm that sold unprocessed, certified goat's milk. She immediately started her baby on our goat's milk formula with cod liver oil and flaxseed oil. She added liquid garlic and some colloidal silver to fight the infection naturally. Because of the previous extensive use of an antibiotic, and because such prescriptions kill all the "friendly" bacteria in the colon too, she also gave her baby some powdered acidophilus. She chose to take her child off the antibiotics while doing this. (Note: Always consult with your doctor before taking any medical steps with your child.)

Two weeks later I spoke with her again. The ear infection was gone. And to this day (it's been months), there is one more happy, healthy, antibiotic-and-ear-infection-free little child enjoying optimum health.

I know that ear infections are always frightening to parents. And they cause so much pain to the child. They're usually treated with antibiotics because the infection develops behind the eardrum, often because of a mucus-like buildup of fluid in which the bacteria grow. This causes pressure on the eardrum. Antibiotics may be the only solution as this progresses. However, not all earaches are due to bacteria. Perhaps your child has a food allergy, which was the case with Daniel (he obviously had several).

To be sure, and to aid in prevention, you can simply avoid feeding your child certain things. Here's a short list of no-nos: cow's milk (the number one culprit), peanut butter, eggs, corn, oranges, and wheat. Also, avoid any contact with cigarette smoke, since studies have shown that children who live in households with one or more smokers suffer more ear infections that those in smoke-free homes.[1] In addition, if your child seems to suffer from ear infections often, be sure to keep her away from certain common allergens, such as down comforters and pillows, pet hair and dust-infested carpets, upholstery and draperies. Consider using one of the commercial duct-cleaning companies to purify your air system.

### *Dietary Guidelines for Ear Infection*

*Keep your child well hydrated.* If you are breast-feeding, do so frequently. Offer an older child plenty of steam distilled water, soups, herbal teas and diluted fruit juices.

*Eliminate dairy foods.* Dairy foods thicken and increase mucus, making it more difficult for an infected ear to drain. (Goat milk is OK). Remember, children under twenty-four months need a high-fat diet to ensure proper brain, nerve and myelin formation. Goat's milk and cod liver oil provide that fat.

*Be sure to give only age-appropriate dosages of nutritional supplements.* You may find the following helpful when dealing with your child's ear infection problems:

> *Lactobacillus acidophilus* or *bifidus* helps a child who is taking antibiotics, who has chronic ear infections or who has an ear infection with a stomachache. In addition to killing infectious bacteria, antibiotics strip the body of necessary friendly bacteria in the intestinal tract. Replace the friendly bacteria by giving your child a high-quality acidophilus product after administering the antibiotic. (We offer an excellent product called, Probiotic Blend; call our office to order 800-726-1834)

> *Vitamin C* and bioflavonoids help with ear infection. They are both mildly anti-inflammatory. Give a child over four years old one dose, six times daily. Select a product that contains mineral ascorbate-buffered vitamin C but no sugar. For younger children, purchase a vitamin C supplement made specifically for infants and toddlers.

> *Zinc* boosts the immune response and helps reduce infection. Give your child zinc-based lozenges, two to three times daily as needed, for a total of one dose of zinc a day. Excessive amounts of zinc can result in nausea and vomiting. Be careful not to exceed the recommended dosage.

> *Colloidal silver*, use ½ dose suggested on the bottle, works great as a natural antibiotic.[2]

## *Allergies*

Yes, earaches may stem from allergies, along with any number of symptoms, such as the sore bottom and diarrhea that Daniel had. And of course, you know about the stuffy noses, sniffling and watery eyes, which are the standard symptoms of most allergies.

But what, exactly, is an allergy? And how can eating right help prevent allergies? First, remember that an allergy is different from an "adverse food reaction" or food sensitivity. For example, you may notice that after most meals your little Johnny suffers from stomach, gas, watery stools and irritability. You may suspect an allergy, but these symptoms could indicate lactose intolerance due to the milk he usually drinks with his food. Taking him off all dairy and milk sugar products will solve the problem. Again, goat's milk can be a replacement.

With a true food allergy the body's immune system is making a defensive mistake. It's trying to ward off certain food proteins as if they were germs. The immune system doesn't get involved in adverse reactions to food, nor does it play a role in the kind of reactions to food additives and colorings that caused little Daniel's rashes and sores. But with an allergy, the immune system is reacting to a certain protein. When this happens, it produces an antibody (an immunoglobulin) to the protein, which then builds up in the body. Every time a person is then exposed to the particular protein, which comes from a certain food, the body releases histamine, which in turn causes all the standard symptoms. (That's why people take antihistamines to counteract the histamine reaction). It's a swirling cycle of suffering.

Allergies are difficult to deal with, but by limiting certain foods from a child's diet you can prevent a lot of suffering. The truly good news is that if you're pregnant you can begin taking childhood allergy-preventing steps right away. Here's what the American Academy of Pediatrics recommends:

Do the following to prevent or delay food allergies in infants at high risk, (such as those with a family history):

> Do not restrict any potentially allergenic foods during pregnancy (however your doctor may suggest that you avoid known trigger foods)

> Breast-feed exclusively for the first six months or use a low-allergenic formula (no cow's milk or soy protein) as recommended by your pediatrician. (Again, we recommend raw, certified goat's milk.)

> Eliminate nuts and peanuts from the mother's diet, and possibly eggs and cow's milk. (We have found that the use of organic health food eggs usually doesn't cause any problem.)

> Delay the introduction of solid foods until six months of age.[3]

In general, to treat an allergy, just identify and remove the allergens. Your child's doctor can administer one of several tests to accomplish this: scratch testing (placing a small amount of diluted allergen on a lightly scratched area of skin); intradermal testing (receiving an injection with suspected allergens; it's more accurate than scratch testing); and blood testing (which measures total and specific levels of IgE and IgG, the antibodies produced by the immune system). The hopeful aspect of allergies is this: They are often outgrown by age seven. Until then, keep helping your child eat right.

### *Asthma*
This life-threatening allergic reaction affects approximately 5 percent of the population, half of whom are children. Asthma

occurs most commonly in children under ten years age, with twice as many males being affected.

The most alarming thing about asthma is that it is on the rise. There has been an 8 percent increase in the prevalence and incidence of asthma since 1980.[4] Since then, the mortality rate from asthma has increased 300 percent in total, and 200 percent in children. There is also a 200 percent increase in the risk of death due to asthma in African American children as compared to Caucasian children.

Many researchers believe that air pollution, chemicals in our diets and the antibiotic weakening of our immune systems are significant causes. Also suspect in the increase of asthma is the parallel increase in the presence of indoor house-mite infestation, indoor natural gas, chemical household products and furniture filled with synthetic material. One more thing: Our "prescription-happy" society is surely contributing to the rise in asthma cases. Asthma is an immune-deficient condition, and strong antibiotics tend to suppress the immune system further.

What can a parent do? Diet can certainly play a role in preventing or overcoming asthma: "The food allergy/asthma link is well known, including dairy products and eggs, and especially foods containing monosodium glutamate (MSG) and sulfitic agents used widely in wine, beer, and snacks. Certain medications, including aspirin, can also provoke asthma."[5] Again, regulate your child's eating to keep them healthy! Also, vitamin B6, vitamin C, B-complex vitamins, vitamin E and essential fats, such as flaxseed oil, and cod liver oil along with a good multi-vitamin, seem to help in most cases.

### *Hyperactivity*
Here's another childhood problem often related to diet. It's likely the expression of either hypoglycemia or food allergies, or both. Sometimes doctors will treat it with a drug called Ritalin.

Drugs such as Ritalin have side effects that include insomnia, rashes, headache and nervousness. Most doctors will warn of these side effects, but some parents are so desperate that they'll try anything. I can't tell you what to do, but I would never put my child on a drug like this. (My husband has an excellent book on this problem. You may call the number listed at the back of this book for more information.)

The main thing is to get the child's diet straightened out. If he is really hyperactive, you can usually tell by observing certain signs. The constant display of extraordinary aggressiveness, destructiveness, bad temper and learning disorders are all signs that may indicate low blood sugar, or hypoglycemia.

Studies have found that a diet that includes caffeine, highly processed foods, red and blue dyes, cow's milk and high-sugar foods are the main cause for hyperactivity in children. Now, there are other reasons out there, so always check with your doctor to be sure. But again, studies have found that 80 to 90 percent of children improve with a proper diet.

### *Attention-deficit hyperactivity disorder (ADHD)*
When I began writing and speaking about health and nutrition, ADHD wasn't even a subject that needed addressing. Most problems that children were experiencing back then, when my husband was seeing up to forty people a day for nutritional counseling, were corrected by changing the family's diet. Today, America is one of the few countries with a significant population of kids who suffer from this disorder. Some countries' native languages don't even have a term for children who are "out of control"—because they haven't experienced it! Before you spend time and money on delving into this subject, first make sure the problem with your child is not due to a lack of consistent discipline. When I say *consistent*, I don't mean telling a child ten times to do something before you follow through with

proper discipline. If that is not the issue, next look at your child's diet.

And please, before you put your child on a drug like Ritalin, start eliminating foods that cause food-sensitivity reactions in hyperactive children:

- Red dye
- blue dye
- coloring and preservatives
- cow's milk
- chocolate
- honey
- corn sweeteners
- fruit juice

If your child appears to have symptoms pointing to ADHD, I suggest ordering a special book from our office. Because of the extensive problems associated with ADHD and the use of Ritalin, and because of the controversial nature of this topic, my husband, Ted, has written a book on this subject. It covers the issues of ADHD, Ritalin and other drugs administered to our young people today. I highly recommend this book for anyone with children on these drugs or for any parent who is interested in improving her child's attitude, behavior and grades in school. Just call 1-800-726-1834 to order your copy.

### *Childhood Obesity*

In light of the problems surveyed above, you might think we've already plumbed the depths of food-related health concerns in kids—far from it! We must address the greatest problem of all: Many of our kids are too fat.

How do doctors determine if your child has a weight problem?

Typically, they glance at a standard height/weight chart and see where your child fits into the normal range. He is deemed:

- Overweight, if his weight is 10 to 20 percent higher than normal.
- Obese, if he is 20 percent or more above normal weight.
- Morbidly obese, if his weight is 50 to 100 percent over normal weight.

Today we face a national problem with overweight children. Studies are now showing that young children weigh much more today compared to children of the same age ten and twenty years ago. Remember, fat cells start developing during infancy and primarily during the first two years of life. Pudgy babies may be perfectly healthy, but not necessarily so. Time will soon tell.

But do you really find the problem of overweight children surprising? If so, here's a suggestion: take a look out your living room window tomorrow morning around 7:00 a.m. See those kids heading for the school bus stop? What else do you see? I'll tell you what I've observed at some bus stops over the years. Early in the morning I see children walking by while eating doughnuts and drinking soda pop. I see candy bars and bubble gum, potato chips and jellybeans. I see a lot of overweight children. Of course, numerous studies bear out what I'm saying about our kids' obesity problems. But as Joseph Piscatella put it in *Fat-Proof Your Child:*

> It doesn't take sophisticated studies alone to show a weight problem exists. The evidence is observational as well. Consider the following: Many grade schools, particularly those in rural areas, have been

using classroom desks made in the 1940's. They can no longer do so. It seems that the increasing size of the young American posterior prevents many of today's grade-school students from fitting the school desk of 50 years ago!

Jeans, the uniform of American youth, have grown larger. A major manufacturer has again re-cut dies to accommodate the increasingly larger sizes of American children and adolescents.[6]

The U.S. Census Bureau says that each year we go through 850 thousand tons of cocoa beans in the form of candies, cakes, cookies, ice cream and beverages. All these things are loaded with saturated fat, sugar, caffeine, chemicals and empty calories. What does this tell you about the American diet? We are poisoning our kids.

### *Adolescent Obesity*

Obese teenagers will probably become obese adults. As a parent, you can do several things to help them control their weight:

- Create a positive attitude about eating so that your children regard food as a friend that makes them healthy rather than a foe that makes them fat.
- Create a positive mealtime environment that is relaxed and healthy.

34

- Remove sugary and fatty snacks from your kitchen cupboard and refrigerator, including all bread, dairy products, pizza, pasta and white rice. (Remember, raw, certified goat's milk is OK, but be careful it does contain a lot of calories—especially for oversized teenagers.)
- Encourage your teenager to get daily exercise; exercise along with him. Find a sport that they enjoy to help them get the proper exercise.
- Avoid being critical. If you show too much concern, your teenager is probably going to be more resistant to losing weight. Keep your distance, but be supportive. The best thing you can do is not to have junk food in the house. I've never seen a two-or-four-year old, or even a twelve-year-old, drive to the food store and bring home junk food. We parents, or well-meaning friends, pick up junk food and bring it home. Let's start thinking about how our decisions affect our children.[8]

### *Keep It Away*

How do we avoid the temptation to "eat wrong"? How can we not contribute to the obesity problem in our families? When we have children at home, we are responsible for feeding them the right foods. The best strategy is the simplest: Just don't bring it home from the grocery store.

I'm speaking from firsthand experience here. If bad stuff ends up in my freezer or refrigerator, it will "call me" until I eat it and make it go away. It just tastes too good.

My husband has spoken several times at seminars with a lady who owns a company that manufactures cookies made with natural ingredients. This sweet and considerate friend would always send Ted home with some of her cookies or brownies. One day, Ted came home from the airport with a big white box. He walked into the kitchen, opened the box and displayed the contents—a dozen of the most beautiful brownies I'd ever seen. They were large and thick with lots of nuts on top. My husband was so cute when he proudly said, "I did not eat even one." *Thanks a lot,* I thought. *Now they're going to call me every day until they're totally consumed.* I did have a plan though. I thought that by putting those beautiful brown temptations out in our guesthouse refrigerator I'd have no problem resisting them. Boy, was I wrong. (Remember—I used to be extremely addicted to chocolate.) Those brownies called out to me every day until finally I'd eaten all of them. I felt terrible, and to make things worse, I ended up with a yeast infection from all that sugar. Shall we say that I reaped what I sowed?

I have the same temptations everyone has. And our kids have them too. Parents, we must help them; their health and happiness depend on it. If we don't want our little ones to look like the cute little Pillsbury Doughboy, then we've got to stop feeding them white, gooey bread, sugary snack cakes and high-fat dairy products. When we start them off right with the best kinds of foods, their good eating habits will follow them throughout a lifetime. It's a principle long recognized:

Train up a child in the way he should go: and when he is
old, he will not depart from it.
--Proverbs 22:6

### *Eating Patterns*

Examine your children's eating patterns and determine whether they need to change. To treat obesity, look at the following issues:

- On average, do your children eat the right amount of food based on their energy requirements?

- When do your children eat the most, at meals or in between?
- Are they drinking too many high-calorie beverages? (Don't permit soft drinks or fruit juices if they are overweight.)
- Is there a relationship between when they eat and what they are doing?
- Are they moving around? Playing sports?
- Is there a relationship between their eating habits and their emotions? [9]

## *Rita and Daniel: A Happy Ending*

Now it's time to finish the story of Rita and her sick little Daniel. Remember them from the beginning of this section? Her toddler was extremely ill; in fact, Rita recently thought that Daniel was going to die. But again, I'll let her tell it...

In less than thirty days I had a different child. In fact, during the first week of trying the Broer's Eat, Drink and Be Healthy program, Daniel's runny nose and ear pulling had completely disappeared. By the second week, his diarrhea, fevers and rashes—everything—were disappearing. I told a neighbor lady about it, and she said "Oh well, he's just outgrowing it." I said, "C'mon. He's outgrowing it in a week?" Then my whole family went on the program.

## *We Thought We Were Normal*

Here's what was wrong with Daniel: the things being fed into his body, from the day he started the flu medicine from the drug store. I admit, at the time, I knew next to nothing about how to feed little Daniel right, once he was weaned. At two years old he'd been living on whole cow's milk, TV dinners and other processed foods.

So, what had the Broer's told us to do on that incredible day when we first visited? It's simple: They put him on their Eat, Drink and Be Healthy program (available at www.healthmasters.com or 800-726-1834). We listened to all the nutrition tapes and started feeding our son and our entire family the recipes out of Sharon's cookbook. The key, though, was taking him off the Top Ten Foods Never to Eat (see page 49 for this Top Ten list.) They put Daniel on their natural vitamin and mineral supplements, plus they made sure we gave him a "protein shake" every day (see page 76 for recipe). Basically, the Broer's changed our family's diet.

That's right! We changed our eating habits, and we began taking the supplements they provided through their office. As a result, my whole family's health picture began to change rapidly within a month. My daughter no longer had chronic headaches and stomachaches, which she'd been having frequently at school. (This is a little child who loves school and cries if she doesn't get to go. But she'd been calling every third day for Mommy to come and get her.)

My husband had recently started wearing glasses at that time. He was also having serious blood pressure problems and backaches. I was experiencing depression and was tired all the time. It seemed that like I had to sleep twelve to fourteen hours a day. But here's the thing: We thought we were normal.

Can you relate to that? When we filled out job applications, we always marked "excellent health" because we didn't have a major disease. We didn't realize until we started feeling good and full of energy how bad we'd been feeling most of our lives. This new process of changing our diet and getting on a healthy vitamin supplement program made all the difference in our energy and attitudes.

And yes, we prayerfully canceled Daniel's ear surgery. I still have two letters in my files from the doctor's office saying things like, "We are worried about Daniel. It's been a couple of weeks since you have been in. Surely he must be ready for new allergy shots. Why did you cancel the surgery?" Sharon Broer didn't tell me to do any of this. I did it on my own, because I saw such tremendous results so rapidly. I just figured that I'd given the doctors two years and hadn't seen any changes. But here we were, after two weeks, with tremendous results. So weighing the two options, I went ahead and dropped the allergy shots in the garbage. I haven't given Daniel a single one.

I have a friend with twin boys who went through a similar thing with ear infections. Her children are now eight years old. They started out with so many of the symptoms Daniel had during those two years. She told me that, of course, these children have had tubes in their ears from their surgeries after all these years. They've actually had one surgery after another and nothing but trouble and sickness. Those two boys take allergy shots and have to keep increasing the dosage as they continue to get worse. It breaks my heart. I believe that through prayer and wise nutritional counsel, we were saved from all of that.

### *It's Not Just for the Little Guys*

A few people have said to me, "Well, Rita, you know that Daniel is just a little guy. It's easy to change somebody that small."

But I have a ten-year-old daughter and it was not easy to change her. In fact, the changes in her health have caused quite a sensation in her school. Everybody notices when she comes into the cafeteria with her bottled water and her bag of fruit and vegetables. The other kids are munching chips and guzzling cokes. But Sarah looks great and feels great. Also, we've seen tremendous changes in other people's lives, folks who've listened to our story and taken it to heart.

Now we have this healthy three-year-old little boy. My husband doesn't have to wear glasses anymore. He doesn't have any more high blood pressure attacks. I am not depressed anymore, and I have loads of energy. My little girl is in school every day without a stomachache.

\* \* \* \* \* \* \* \* \* \* \* \* \* \* \* \* \* \* \* \* \* \* \* \* \* \* \* \* \* \* \* \* \* \* \* \* \*

*Rita's story has inspired me to continue championing good nutrition for families. I hope it will inspire you to keep reading this book. If you're a parent—or if you hope to be one any time soon—then please read on! The things you know (or don't know) about the food you eat will make all the difference to your child's health—and your health also.*

# 2

✳✳✳✳✳✳✳

# *Who's Telling Them What to Eat?*

OVER IN MERRY old England they call it the "telly." We've got our own names for that noisy, ever-present guest in our living rooms: the tube, the TV, even "home entertainment center." Whatever you call it at your house, have you noticed how much it's...well, there? How often it's blaring in the background as you talk with your family? As you answer the phone? As you sit down to eat? And what is the telly telling? Fact is, it's telling our kids what to eat, day in and day out. Sandwiched between every seven-minute slice of *The Power Rangers* come a variety of thoroughly entertaining food commercials. With movie-quality sound, full-color animations and the highest-tech production values, these ads tell our kids how good it'll feel to load up on junk. I must admit, though, from a marketing perspective, the packaging is pretty nifty.

### *What Television Doesn't Tell You*

The boob-tube doesn't tell you how bad it is for your child to be eating Fried Wonders, Sticky Goo-Goo's and Creemie Cakes. Most of the loudly touted fare is little more than a colorful mixture of fat and sugar, usually with a "luscious cream-filled center." You might as well call your kids over to the kitchen counter, make them open wide and funnel a few quarts of sugar, lard, artificial flavors and dyes right into their bellies. Or give them a couple injections of melted Crisco. Or...I could go on, but you get the picture. This is bad medicine, no matter how it goes down.

### *Limit the Influence of TV!*

Like it or not, television has a major impact on most of our lives. The Stevens family had a single television set, and when it broke, they never got around to having it fixed. For a year and a half, they lived without television and didn't miss it.

Then Naomi's mother came to stay with the family for a few months between the time her house was sold and her new condominium was ready. She brought her TV with her.

"All of a sudden, I found myself alone in the kitchen making dinner every night," Naomi said. "Before, everyone used to help with setting the table and cooking. After dinner, we would sit around the table and talk for a while."

"When that TV came into the house, the kids raced into the den and argued over what show they would watch. I was glad when

42

Mom's condo was finally ready. We could get back to being a family that talked again."[1]

Moms and Dads, our children are being brainwashed today. The average preschooler watches twenty-six hours of TV per week. Kids ages six to sixteen watch twenty-four hours of TV per week. The average American child between the ages of two and eleven views over twenty thousand TV commercials. (I don't call them commercials; I call them "brainwashers," because that's what they're doing.) The message is, "Hey kids! Eat low-fiber, high-sugar, highly refined junk foods!" Those little children sit there so innocently, and then they will go and nag their parents at the grocery store until they buy them the longed-for item. Often it's not because they even want the food. They want the toy in the box. (Don't you think these advertisers realize what they are doing?) We give in and say, "Ok, you can have these a couple of times a week." Then the child gets sicker and sicker. It is a vicious cycle. We have a rule in our house that whenever a TV commercial comes on, we mute the volume, via the remote control. In fact, we make it a game to se who can mute the commercial first. It really helps to eliminate a lot of the unnecessary noise and trash commercials from our home.

No, the advertisers aren't concerned about your child's health. I would like you to spend a month watching the commercials that come with the cartoons. See how many advertised foods are high in nutrition on these commercials. There are none. The advertisers want to sell their products, while most of the time, their product is a high-sugar, high-calorie, low-fiber, refined non-food. That is what I call 100 percent junk food.

In a recent study, 40 percent of the parents questioned said they had nothing to do with their children's breakfast every single day. You can't build healthy cells from a snack cake and cola for breakfast, but that is what television tells us. Simply stated, TV is fattening. Kids in America spend three, four, even five hours a day gazing at those flickering images. During those long hours they scarcely move, let alone do any exercise except to grab another snack. And along with the cartoons and cops and comedies comes a liberal dose of advertising. It's hard to think about fruits and vegetables when you're invited to gorge on Cookie Crisp cereal, Hostess Twinkies and hot dogs guaranteed to plump your kids.

What can you do? First, try to wean your children off the tube by setting certain times for viewing and establishing limits on the number of hours per day and per week. For many Americans, not only children, television becomes addicting. They sit in front of the set to watch a given show and don't stand up again until its bedtime. The same goes for the kids. They turn on the tube on Saturday morning to watch a particular cartoon, and before you know it, they're glued to the TV for many hours. Experts say that we should never allow a child under the age of two to watch television at all. It may actually affect the brain's development. This is especially true at younger ages when learning to talk and play with others is so important.[2]

## *Real TV: Processed Foods and Sick Kids*

This is the sickest generation of children we've ever had. The biggest reason, based on my observation and research, is that our children are being raised on processed foods. Kids are developing degenerative diseases they never had back at the turn of the century. Years ago, we'd rarely hear of a child with cancer and diabetes, which are so prevalent today among our youth. Today, America ranks very high among other nations in incidences of attention-deficit hyperactivity disorder, cancer and sudden infant death syndrome, while scholastic scores have plummeted over the past four decades.

Kids' bodies aren't made to live on these processed foods, so their health is deteriorating. Specifically, what are the problems with processing?  I'll save a discussion of additives and dyes for the next section.  For now, take a quick look at these five processing hazards:

### *Sugar blues*

Sugar is just plain addictive, like television.  Put the two together, and your kids are playing in the middle of a street called Poor Health.  And what's in that cereal so heavily peddled in prime time?  There is *so* much sugar in the favorite cereals of children.  In Alpha-Bits there is 38 percent sugar.  Frosted Flakes cereal is 41 percent sugar.  Life cereal is 16 percent sugar.  Bran Flakes cereal (which you might think had no sugar at all) is 13 percent sugar.  And how about Sugar Smacks?  61 percent!  Many studies have shown that children whose breakfasts are nutritionally inadequate perform at lower levels in school.  There is a definite correlation between diet and a child's grades.

Consider the case of Tommy.  He's feeling blue today and has a mild headache.  He's a third-grader sitting in his classroom, and he is very unhappy.  He's staring out the window, hardly paying attention.  It just so happens that today, Tommy's teacher is talking about his favorite subject, math.  *What's wrong with Tommy?*  His teacher wonders.  *Is he sick?  Is he undergoing some type of emotional problem today?*  Tommy had his usual breakfast this morning:  two doughnuts and a can of cola.  In that cola alone, Tommy got a mega dose of caffeine and about ten teaspoons of sugar.  He was bound to "come down" from that intense stimulation.  Tommy usually has trouble getting up on time in the morning, and then he runs out of the house to the bus stop every day, grabbing his standard breakfast.  When his parents (who tend to sleep in too long themselves) call after him, "Tommy, did you eat your breakfast?" he replies, "Oh, sure I did."  Tommy is a nutritional disaster waiting to happen—in the form of future obesity, heart disease, even cancer.  But his parents continue to feel satisfied:  At least he's eating before school.

## Sugar: The Bad News

According to Dr. Earl Mindell, in 1987 the average American was consuming over 125 pounds of sugar each year. Today, it's closer to 165 pounds per person. What's so bad about sugar? Mindell lists problems like these:

- It causes tooth decay
- It contributes to obesity
- It aggravates asthma, mental illness and nervous disorders
- It increases the possibility of heart disease, diabetes, hypertension, gallstones, back problems, arthritis and hypoglycemia
- It causes loss of essential nutrients
- It potentiates salt to raise blood pressure
- It imbalances the body's calcium/phosphorous ration

*Watch out for sugar!*[3]

### Pesticide and residue dangers

Our processed foods come with poisons in them. Consider all those "fruit-filled" juices and snacks for the kids. The Food and Drug Administration tests very little produce for chemical residues. Tested items with illegal quantities of toxins and also residues of banned chemicals are still ending up on our dinner tables. Pesticides abound on produce imported for other countries.

Consumers, and the resulting toxic effects base tolerances for the use of pesticides on food crops, on estimates of the amount of pesticide that may be ingested. According to the National Academy of Sciences (NAS), the actual risk of developing cancer due to toxic pesticide residues is much higher than the EPA standards permit or than federal health and safety officials admit.

Three chemicals in particular stand out as major problems:

1. ***Methyl parathion*** is an insecticide in the family known as organophosphates, often found on domestic peaches, green beans, apples and pears. "Organophosphates are all designed to be neurological poisons," explains Dr. Philip Landrigan, chairman of the department of community and preventative medicine at Mount Sinai School of Medicine in New York. "They work fundamentally the same in humans as in insects."[4] In 1998 the Environmental Protection Agency (EPA) concluded that methyl parathion posed an "unacceptable risk" as currently used. One study found that residue levels consistently exceeded the EPA's safe daily limit for the average five-year old child.

2. ***Dieldrin*** was removed from the market in 1974, but this carcinogenic pesticide takes decades to disappear from the soil. When the USDA tested winter squash in 1997, dieldrin showed up in three-quarters of the frozen samples. Two-thirds of the positive samples exceeded the safe daily limit for a young child. Dieldrin is absorbed into the pulp of the vegetable, making it impossible to wash off.

3. ***Aldicarb*** is the most toxic pesticide. Many growers stopped using it in 1990, but some potato growers in Washington and Idaho resumed in 1996. Its use is on the increase. The USDA tested 160 individual potatoes from positive samples in 1997. About 1 in 20 had more than the safe limit for a young child. This toxin also gets under the skin of produce and can't be washed off.

Today in the United States the numbers and use of agricultural toxic chemicals have skyrocketed. But I'm not just referring to what's sprayed on our food; it's also what's applied to the nutrient-void soil. Even though many pesticides have been banned or restricted due to the risks they pose to consumer health, they are still found on our foods. The FDA lacks effective procedures and authority to enforce the regulations. Here's my point: The United States has the highest infant death rate of any industrialized nation. Parents, *please* consider buying organically grown produce, which is increasingly available. Avoid the processed junk food whose fruit is suspect.

### *Some Scary Facts*

I dislike scaring my friends, but sometimes the facts are, indeed, fearful. Did you know that?

- Tranquilizing drugs are injected into many pigs immediately before transport to slaughter—making a withdrawal period impossible and giving diners unexpected sedation with their pork dish?[5]
- Sixty percent of all herbicides, 90 percent of all fungicides and 30 percent of all insecticides cause cancer?[6]
- Pesticides are one type of indirect food additive of concern, but another involves residues from animal drugs? The FDA has been trying to rein in the use of antibiotics in animal feed since 1972, but cattle and poultry are still being fed antibiotic feed to increase their growth. More and more antibiotic-resistant infections in humans are occurring, and scientists worldwide are blaming "animal husbandry practices" as an important cause.[7]
- Consumers and scientists have been fighting for more than two decades to stop hormones being used to increase the growth of cattle, swine and poultry? But these powerful drugs are still widely employed. It is not just estrogen added directly to the food supply that may have adverse effects. The EPA announced in October 1993 some emerging evidence indicating that the insecticide

48

endosulfan and other chemicals that imitate estrogen may be associated with instances of breast cancer.[8]

### Sodium nitrite risks

Preserved, high-fat luncheon meats provide us with a deadly, cancer-producing threat. Pork products such as sausage, ham, bacon, pepperoni and hot dogs top the list of foods to avoid. They are preserved with nitrites, proven carcinogens. Sodium nitrite reacts with your child's stomach acids to form nitrosamines, which my husband, Ted, has called "one of the most potent cancer-causing agents known to man." He goes on to say:

This chemical is so lethal that a pregnant woman can increase the risk of brain cancer in her infant, by eating hot dogs combined with diet sodas, containing nutrasweet or aspartame. Why are these products still on our grocery market shelves? The sad truth is that we have some serious health problems in this country that are not being addressed by the federal government.... No one cares about your well-being and the well-being of your loved ones as you do, so the ultimate responsibility is yours. I heard an old Baptist preacher say one time that every pot sits on its own bottom.[9]

### Antibiotic perils

The simple fact is that many of our processed dairy products are made with milk produced from cows...on drugs. The antibiotics help keep the cows from getting sick. But as they do with any drug, bacteria constantly grow into new drug-resistant strains. The antibiotics must then be changed or dosages increased. All of this creates a vicious cycle: more drugs, more resistance, more drugs. Here's a sad fact: *Newsweek* reported in 1992 that "13,300 hospital patients died of infections that resisted every drug doctors tried."[10]

There's no doubt that antibiotics were a boon to civilization when Alexander Fleming discovered penicillin. But their proliferation in our processed foods is a definite peril. If you'd like to do more in-depth study on the antibiotic problem, I highly recommend that you spend a day in your public library looking it up.

## *Medicine and Your Taste Buds*

Did you know that certain prescription drugs make it difficult to taste food? Check the examples below. The good news: Your sense of taste usually returns when you stop taking the drug.

- Captopril (Capoten) a drug to lower blood pressure
- Griseofulvin (Fulvicin, Grifulvin, Grisactin, Gris-PEG) an anti-fungus drug
- Lithium (Cibalith-S, Eskalith, Lithobid, Lithonate, Lithotabs) an anti-depressant/anti-manic drug
- Metronidazole (Flagyl) an anti-infective drug
- Penicillamine (Cuprimine, Depen) an anti-rheumatic
- Rifampin (Rifadin, Rimactane) an anti-tuberculosis drug[10]

### *Cholesterol complications*
Cholesterol is a waxy substance that flows in the bloodstream. It comes from animal-source foods, while foods from plant sources contain none. Some of the highest cholesterol deliverers are eggs, cheese and liver. We do need some cholesterol in our bodies so we can produce hormones that form the sheaths around our nerves, but our livers produce all the cholesterol we need for this purpose. The overabundance we get from processed foods can only hurt us, and our children. "Statistics show that about 30 to 40 percent of children in families with a history of heart disease have high blood cholesterol and that up to 80 percent of them will carry it into adulthood. Also, autopsies performed on 88 children who had died from other causes showed that almost

40 percent of them had the first signs of heart disease, which is fibrous plaque or fatty deposits in the walls of their blood vessels."[11] These are truly chilling and heartbreaking statements aren't they?

Help your kids stay away from high-fat, high-cholesterol junk food (no matter how good it looks on TV)! High-quality organic eggs are fine, and they are a great source of protein—as long as your child is getting a good diet that doesn't consist primarily of high-cholesterol junk foods.

### *Stay Away From This "Top Ten List"*

Actually, there are at least ten food items your kids should avoid—and the first four on the list they should never consume in their lifetimes. So here's your Top Ten List of things (from my husband's book, *Maximum Energy*) that should sink to rock-bottom on your grocery list—before you erase them completely:

1. *Pork and high-fat luncheon meats.* They are loaded with nitrates, artificial dyes and chemicals; they can also cause parasite infection.

2. *Shellfish: lobster, crab, oysters, clams and shrimp.* They can contain abnormally high levels of arsenic, lead and mercury.

3. *All hydrogenated oils, including margarine and shortening products.* These increase the risk of heart disease and cancer. Use organic butter, Macadamia Nut Oil, Grape Seed Oil, Virgin Coconut Oil or olive oil instead.

4. *Aspartame (NutraSweet) and Splenda.* Never use these artificial sweetener products.

5. *"Junk foods," all high fat, high-sugar, chemically processed snacks.*

6. *High-fat dairy products.* Goat's milk is fine.

7. *Soy products and Monosodium Glutamate (MSG)*

8. *Caffeine.* Limit your intake of caffeinated products.

9. *Chlorine and fluoride.* These chemicals are found in treated water supplies. Use reverse-osmosis or steam-distilled water.

10. *Alcohol products.* Alcohol destroys brain cells and increases the risk of pancreatic cancer, alcoholism, liver cancer, breast cancer, osteoporosis and cirrhosis of the liver.

My husband has written an entire book, titled *Maximum Energy that* explains the dangers of these products in detail with hundreds of references. You can order this from our website, www.healthmasters.com, or call our office at 1-800-726-1834 and order it. No matter who's telling your children what to eat, television commercials notwithstanding, make sure your kids avoid that list.

# 3

\*\*\*\*\*\*\*

# *Turn Off the Tube and Start the Day Right!*

I WAS WATCHING a morning talk show that introduced a totally new concept in exercise for children. In the studio a young girl sat on a stationary bike that included a TV screen. The host explained that this was no ordinary stationary bike, since it offered full-color entertainment along with a good workout. You see, the bike was actually the television's power source. No pedal, no picture.

My first reaction was probably just like yours: "How clever." But the more I thought about the concept, the more disturbing the idea became. Why? Because I know that at an American Heart Association conference several years ago, one expert nutritionist reported that in 1993 "commercials for high-fat foods made up 41 percent of total commercials shown on Saturday morning, as compared to 16 percent in 1990."[1] Today, I'm sure the percentage is much higher. In other words, when it comes to pushing nutrition, things are getting worse on TV. And even if your child is pedaling a bike while watching, he's still being indoctrinated with ideas that could have serious effects on his health for years to come.

### *Champion a Better Breakfast*

Television thrills our kids with the breakfast of champions, but breakfast is kind of a joke today in America. It's the one meal of the day that most people skip. Yet I call it our "Fuel Meal." Breakfast should consist of "live food" that gives our bodies fuel for the remainder of the day. Nevertheless, the average American breakfast usually consists of high-sugar boxed cereal, a processed orange-flavored juice and/or processed breakfast bars. This is an ideal breakfast for someone who would like a high-sugar, low-fiber diet—exactly the opposite of what we should be eating to start out the day.

Variety is the key with breakfast, but I really think there are only three main categories for this first meal of the day: Grains (I'm talking about the kind that if you throw them out the door into the soil and add water, they'll grow), fruit and boxed cereals that come direct from the grocer's shelf (which we tend to overuse). Lets look at all three for a moment:

### *Go for the good grains.*
I've found that when people don't know how to make something, they just leave it out of their diets completely. But we can't do that with grains because they're so essential to our good health. We have a tendency to think of raw grains as what comes in the cornflakes and other cereals we buy. But those are overly processed, and I can't call them nutritious grains. When processing is complete, the nutritive value is largely depleted. It only remains to put back numerous synthetic vitamins usually made from coal-tar derivatives (or petroleum by-products). That lets the manufacturer advertise, "Vitamin fortified!" The bottom

line:  The whole mess plugs up the colon and makes you sick over the years.

The early 1900's brought us the marvelous invention of the roller mill.  But we're having some problems because of that nice little machine.  It was intended to mill our grains, which strips them of vital nutrients.  The bran layer is removed, and this leaves us with a lot of empty calories—which become our boxed cereals of today.  Mom, if you're feeding your child a popular boxed cereal, you need to hear this:  A study was done several years ago with rats, cereals and the boxes they came in.  The researchers concluded that the boxes had more fiber than the stuff inside!

### *Highest Fiber?*

Foods high in fiber:  Grains, bran, seeds, nuts, many fruits and vegetables.

Three fruits high in fiber, from the highest down:  Mango, apple, and strawberries.

Vegetables with the highest fiber content:  Green leafy vegetables.  Carrots are next highest. In contrast, whole grains are loaded with B vitamins, which regulate the nervous system.  They're loaded with fiber, too.  Just yesterday I was reading through my latest catalog from our natural foods source and saw a new cereal called Simply Fiber. It has 14 grams of fiber per serving—that's high!  I suggest you make a hot cereal out of your whole grains.  If you use boxed cereals occasionally, go for the cereal with more than 6 or 7 grams of fiber per serving. There are some good granola cereals on the market that you can find in whole-food markets.

Remember that fiber is the part of the plant food that is not digested.  That's why we call it roughage.  We need 24 to 25 grams of fiber every day. That's a lot more than we're getting. The average American normally gets 6 to 8 grams per day. Can you see why we're having so many problems today in America? An internationally known doctor, Dennis Burkett, suggested that one of the biggest causes for the major health problems today in America and other Western nations is due to our reduced fiber intake. He attributed much of our heart disease, obesity, colon cancer, varicose veins, appendicitis, constipation, gallstones and diverticulitis to the lack of fiber in our diets. (Note: Bran is a high source of fiber. Advertisers have really overused the word, of course; if they put "bran" in their product's name, it will sell regardless of how much, if any, bran the product contains.)

### Go ahead, have some fruit.
Having fruit for breakfast is important because fruit is a highly concentrated carbohydrate and is good for you. It's good to eat fruit before 2:00 p.m. if you can, because it does give you a lot of energy. If you just want to have an all-fruit breakfast, at least try to eat three different fruits that day, because variety is critical. Why? Varying the fruits you eat means you're getting a large amount of different trace minerals in your system. If you eat a good whole-grain cereal, then use fresh fruit as a topping.

### No! Not that boxed stuff!
Before you picked up this manual, how many of you would honestly give your child a chocolate candy bar for breakfast? Well, maybe I shouldn't ask that question. I've seen it done. But here's the thing: There is less sugar per ounce in some candy bars than there is in some breakfast cereals! For instance, you'll find 5 teaspoons of sugar in a Milky Way candy bar but 16 teaspoons of sugar in a cup of Frosted Flakes or Froot Loops. We wouldn't give them a candy bar, but we do push high-sugar cereals at them.

Boxed cereals usually have wheat, oats, barley or corn as one of their bases. The problem? They have to be "fortified" because the natural nutrients have been removed in processing. (Otherwise, there would be no need for fortifying.) Those grains have been crinkled, smashed, puffed, flattened, baked and crushed. By the time it gets to your table, the most useful thing in the box is the toy surprise.

## *Take Another Look at These Cereals!*

Do you know the fiber content in your child's favorite, boxed cereals? One ounce of bran is about 3.6 grams of fiber. Let's compare some cereals to that: One ounce of All-Bran, Bran Buds and Nabisco 100 percent Bran—1.8 to 2.3 grams fiber.

Can you see it? The fiber content is really cut down. Some cereals have half of that amount of fiber: Sugar Pops, Sugar Frosted Flakes, Corn Total, Cocoa Puffs, Post Toasties--.1 to .2 grams of fiber per ounce.

Why are so many little children constipated? If they're constipated at ages four and five, wait until they're twenty-four and twenty-five. They are in trouble!

Now, just a final word about the advertising that says something like, "Extra-fiber, all-bran cereal." If I didn't know any better, I'd think this was all very good, wouldn't you? But if you'll notice, the third or fourth ingredient is corn syrup, which is sugar. Some of these cereals don't want sugar to be the first ingredient, so they'll put the second ingredient as sugar, the fifth ingredient as corn syrup, the sixth ingredient as dextrose (a sugar). They spread it out because they don't want sugar to blare out at you as the primary ingredient, even though it is. And then they pile in the additives.

## *Get the Facts About Those Additives*

Recently, I thought I'd conduct an experiment. I went down to my local grocery store and counted all the child-directed food that contained aspartame (NutraSweet). Wow! I left the store in shock. Here's what I found in my brief, informal survey. I counted several cereals (the ones that appeal to children—with kid pictures, toy offers, chocolate flavors, marshmallows, funny box covers and so forth) and all manner of other products that kids consume, such as puddings, gelatins, breakfast bars, ice cream, sodas, syrups, candies, cookies, dressings, powdered drink mixes...the list goes on. Remember, this artificial sweetener seems to be linked to brain cancer.

I've become so concerned that I definitely want you to learn about additives. The most basic thing to know is that there are two general groupings: (1) direct additives (which include flavorings, preservatives, buffers, neutralizers, stabilizers, texturizers, emulsifiers, colorings and bleachers and sanitizing agents) and (2) indirect additives (which include substances that come from packaging, processing, pesticides and animal drugs).

## *Check Out These Additive Myths*

Most Americans consume about four pounds of additives per year. How much do we understand about them? Here are some common myths:

- "All additives are bad." (Fact: All additives are not bad—at least not all bad. For instance, most preservatives used to prevent the growth of bacteria that cause deadly botulism offer benefits that far outweigh their risks.)
- "Some additives are completely safe." (No additive is completely safe for all people all of the time. The most innocuous additives—even ordinary food, for that

58

matter—are capable of causing adverse reactions during illness, for example, or if ingested while taking certain medications. Also, substances that are harmless for adults can be dangerous for children.)

- "Natural additives are safer than chemical ones." (Not necessarily. Coumarin, from Tonka beans, was used for seventy-five years in flavorings before it was found to cause liver damage.)
- "Naturally preserved meats are safe and chemical free." (Whether done in old smokehouses or new factories, the smoking process produces resinous, cancer-causing chemicals that are imparted to the food.) [2]

I'll focus on the direct additives that you can find on most package labels (later, in section eight, you'll learn more about label reading). Let me do it by just giving you nine guidelines in the form of facts for you to chew on:

### Fact #1. Labels are hard to read.
Finding the ingredients on the label can sometimes be as difficult as reading or pronouncing them. They are hidden under flaps and folds, and the print is sometimes so small you can only read it with a magnifying glass.

### Fact #2. Ingredients are listed on the label by quantity.
The ingredients used in the largest quantity will be listed first, and the ingredients used in the smallest quantity will be listed last.

### Fact #3. Long lists are a warning.
Remember this principle when reading labels: The longer the list of ingredients, the higher probability of chemical additives present in the product.

### Fact #4. "Natural" may be unnatural.

When a product states "All natural ingredients" or "No preservatives added" or "Natural fruit flavors, with real fruit juice," don't be misled. This does not mean the product contains no harmful additives. The manufacturer uses these words to make you feel better about the product.

### Fact #5. Health-food stores aren't perfect.

Realize that just because food is purchased in a whole foods market or health food store does not guarantee the product is free from harmful additives. Always read the label.

### Fact #6. Organic food is worth the money.

Sadly, when nothing is added to foods, they cost us more. Examples: Unbleached flour costs four times more than bleached. Un-sulfured raisins cost six times more than those that are treated. Untreated tomatoes cost five times more than regular canned tomatoes. It may be more expensive to buy organic, but it is worth it for the privilege of not having to consume indirect additives.

### Fact #7. Processing demands additives.

There are more than three thousand common indirect and direct food additives in our diet, nearly two-thirds of them being flavorings used to replace the natural flavors lost during processing.[3]

### Fact #8. Additives and nutrition don't mix.

The majority of food additives have nothing to do with the nutritional value of our food.

### Fact #9. Dozens of additives have been declared unsafe.

As of 1972, there were thirty-five widely used additives that had been approved for human consumption. They have since been removed as unsafe, most of them because they were found to be capable of causing cancer. In 1978, food additives were a $1.3

billion-a-year business. Today, the additive business is more than a $4.5 billion enterprise.[4]

## *What's Protecting You?*

Food additives are extensively studied and regulated, primarily by the FDA. Legislation in 1958 and 1960 required manufacturers to prove the safety of any new additive; before that, the burden was on government to prove the health danger of a substance. Here are three of the standard guidelines:

- *Margin of safety.* Food manufacturers can use only one-hundredth of the least amount of an additive shown to be toxic in lab animals.
- *The Delaney Amendment.* This rule states that a substance shown to cause cancer in animals or man may not be added to food in any amount. Food manufacturers argue against this rule on the grounds that in some cases the cancer risk is low or that any risk is outweighed by the benefits the additive may provide—as with nitrites, saccharin and aspartame, weak carcinogens that are still on the market.
- *Testing for safety.* Even under the best circumstances, the absolute safety of an additive can never be proven. Any substance may be harmful when consumed in excess. Animal studies, which are our primary mode of testing, have limitations. They may not be effective in assessing the degree of cancer risk from long-term use because of the animals' short life spans. Moreover, it is hard to make precise comparisons between animals and humans. Other questions concern possible interactions of the hundreds of additives we consume.[5]

What are the most common additives to avoid? You'd have to become a "student of additives" to know and keep up with all the chemicals and poisons added to our food. So to simplify things,

I'll refer to the most common additives I come across in my weekly grocery shopping. But please note: Once I find any of these additives listed, I don't even waste my time reading the rest of the label; that piece of packaged food is not for me, or my children. Also, if the following additives are present in anything I plan to purchase, I find another brand to buy:

### MSG (monosodium glutamate): Used to intensify meat and spice flavorings

- Reported complaints: headache, chest pains, numbness, irritability and depression
- Brain damage and memory loss
- Baby food companies removed this from baby food. (But why was it in baby food to begin with?)
- Listed under other names: hydrolyzed vegetable protein (HVP)
- "Natural flavorings"

### Aspartame: Used in NutraSweet and Equal, contains the following ingredients"

- *Methanol*—a neurological poison that cannot be made nonpoisonous. It can cause headaches, blindness and permanent brain damage.
- *Aspartic acid*—similar to MSG, it has been known to over-stimulate neural cells, causing cell death. This is why it is called an "excitotoxin." It literally kills brain cells. Studies done by Dr. John Olney, at Washington University School of Medicine at St. Louis, have shown that it leaves "holes" in the brains of tested laboratory animals.
- *Phenylalanine*—causes permanent brain damage if concentrations are high enough.

When aspartame is ingested, the three component parts above are released, causing all of their respective side effects. Dr. Olney has shown that when aspartame is combined with nitrites (found in hot dogs, luncheon meats, bacon and sausage), diketopiperazine can possibly be formed, further degrading to a nitrosourea. Nitrosoureas are the most effective method known for producing malignant brain tumors in experimental animals.

To bring this problem into clarity, a simple example would be combining a pepperoni pizza with a diet soda or bacon and eggs with coffee sweetened with NutraSweet. Perhaps these simple combinations are the answer to the huge increase in malignant brain tumors in both adults and children in this country. Several years ago when the increasing rates of brain cancer came to national attention, cell phones were given the blame. However, children do not use cell phones. I personally believe the problems stem from the use of NutraSweet. With its chemical breakdown and combinations, this surge of brain cancer has become too common.

### Nitrites: Used to give that "pretty pink color" to cured meats, bacon, bologna, hot dogs, ham, Vienna sausages and luncheon meats.

- Nitrites combined with natural stomach acids create nitrosamines, powerful cancer-causing agents.
- Baby food manufacturers voluntarily removed nitrites from baby foods in the early 1970's.
- In 1977, Germany banned nitrites, except in certain species of fish.

### Olestra or Olean

These are the "fake fats" introduced in 1996, a combination of soybean oil and sucrose that has been manipulated into molecules too large to be absorbed or digested by the human body. Preliminary studies found that Olestra caused tumors in laboratory animals. Possible side effects include intestinal cramping and loose stools.

*Monoglycerides and Diglycerides: Synthetic substances made for emulsifying and defoaming agents*
- Used in bakery products to maintain "softness:"
- Used in beverages, ice cream, shortening, margarines, chocolate, whipped toppings and cosmetic crams
- On the FDA list of food additives to be studied for possible reproduction effects

*BHA (butylated hydroxyanisole): A preservative used in many products, including beverages, ice cream, baked goods, potato chips and breakfast cereals.*
- In experiments at Michigan State University, BHA appeared to be less toxic to the kidneys than BHT.
- In November 1990, Glenn Scott, M.D., filed a petition with the FDA asking the agency to prohibit the use of BHA in food.

*BHT (butylated hydroxytoluene): A preservative used in the same type of products as BHA*
- Like BHA, causes complaints of allergic reactions.
- "The possibility that BHT may convert other ingested substances into toxic or cancer-causing agents should be investigated" (from the Select Committee of the Americas for Experimental Biology, which advises the FDA on food additives).
- Prohibited as a food additive in England

*Aluminum*
- Frequently used in food additives, cosmetics and antacids
- Can aggravate kidney and lung disorders
- Aluminum deposits have been found in the brains of Alzheimer's patients

*Aluminum sulfate*
- Used in producing sweet and dill pickles
- Used as an antiseptic, astringent and in detergents and deodorants
- Moderately toxic by ingestion and injection
- May affect reproduction

*Artificial flavorings*
- The largest category of additives: example, natural lemon, benzaldehyde (synthetic)
- More than two thousand flavorings added to foods, approximately five hundred natural and the rest synthetic
- "Natural orange" is methyl salicylate (a synthetic)

***Hydrogenated or partially hydrogenated oil: Used in margarine and Crisco-type products; very "cheap" oils used in chips, crackers, cereal, peanut butter, snack cakes, bread and many more products***
- Makes liquid oil partially solid
- Adversely affects the level of fat in the blood; linked to colon cancer and heart disease

*Other oils to avoid*
- Cottonseed oil
- Palm kernel oil
- Corn oil
- Soybean oil
- Canola oil

*Oils we recommend*
- Regular use—virgin, cold-pressed olive oil, macadamia nut oil, grape seed oil, coconut oil
- Occasional use—good, old-fashioned organic butter

## *Be Careful With Colorings and Dyes*

In 1996, my husband, Ted, my son Austin and I attended a wedding reception. We saw friends we hadn't seen in years. Austin, then seven years old, was checking out the food with his friends. The punch table loomed in a far corner, and the large crystal bowl held some type of bright red liquid. I remember my husband coming over to me and asking, "How much punch has Austin had?"

When Ted asked Austin, he admitted to having consumed four glasses. I went over and looked at the punch and thought, *Oh no, red dye!* Later that night when we got home, Austin's voice was very raspy; for the next three or four days he was blowing his nose constantly. He had a cough for four months. He'd never been exposed to artificial coloring like that, which to his body was a toxin.

## *Artificial Food Colorings (FD and C Colors)*

A color additive is any dye, pigment or other substance capable of coloring food, drugs or cosmetics. Artificial colors offer considerable health risks, with absolutely no known health or nutritional benefits. Here's a brief history…

> 1900—There were more than eighty dyes used to color food. The same dye used to color clothes could be used to color candy.
>
> 1938—Colors were given numbers instead of chemical names. Fifteen colors were used at the time.
>
> 1950—Children were made ill by certain colorings used in candy and popcorn. Since these incidents, Orange No. 1 and 2, Red No. 1 and 32, Violet No. 1 and Yellow No. 1,2,3 and 4 have been de-listed.
>
> 1976—Red No. 2 was removed because it was found to cause tumors in rats. Red No. 4 (the coloring for

maraschino cherries) was banned due to its cancer-causing agents.

\*\*\*\*\*\*\*\*\*\*\*\*\*\*\*\*\*\*\*\*\*\*\*\*\*\*\*\*\*\*\*\*\*\*\*\*\*\*\*\*\*\*\*\*\*\*\*\*\*\*\*\*\*

To experience how quickly your skin absorbs, rub a cut clove of garlic on the bottom of your foot. Within thirty minutes you will taste it in your mouth.

\*\*\*\*\*\*\*\*\*\*\*\*\*\*\*\*\*\*\*\*\*\*\*\*\*\*\*\*\*\*\*\*\*\*\*\*\*\*\*\*\*\*\*\*\*\*\*\*\*\*\*\*\*

Knowing this, I was still shocked when a doctor friend of ours was telling my husband and me about one of her patients. She was running some chemical testing on this patient, trying to find out what was causing some of her problems. When the test results came back, the doctor found unusually high levels of Blue Dye #1. The patient was totally puzzled, because she was so careful to read labels and avoid artificial colorings. After much thought and several questions about the products she'd put on her skin, the patient admitted to the doctor, "You know, I've been washing my dishes every day for the last twenty-five years in blue dishwashing liquid." Mystery solved!

Whatever you do, don't consider it a great loss to give up your favorite snack through better label reading. Look at this as a learning experience. It will help you and those you love avoid putting poisons into your system that could cause a shorter life. Look at this as a "life extender."

### *Overall, Stick to the Clean Stuff*

In the last section, I gave you the Top Ten List of foods to avoid. I'll be talking about "clean" and "unclean" foods in the sections to come, so you need to know what I'm referring to. These are foods the Bible tells us to eat or to avoid. They are biblically forbidden foods referred to in Scripture as "clean" and "unclean."

### *Clean and Unclean Food List*

*Red meat*

        Clean—Beef, lamb, mutton, veal

        Unclean—Pork, dog, cat, horse, mule

*Wild game*

        Clean—Buffalo, caribou, deer, elk, moose

        Unclean—Armadillo, bear, beaver, muskrat, opossum, rabbit, raccoon, squirrel, wild boar, woodchuck

*Poultry/game birds*

        Clean—Capon, chicken, Cornish hen, dove, grouse, lark, partridge, pheasant, pigeon, quail, turkey

        Unclean—Eagle, falcon, goose, osprey

*Seafood*

        Clean—Bass, bluefish, bream, butterfish, cusk, grouper, haddock, hake, halibut, herring, kipper, mullet, pilchard, Pollock, pompano, porgy, red snapper, rosefish, salmon, sardine, sea trout, shad, sole, whiting

        Unclean—Blue marlin, catfish, dolphin, eel, lamprey, mackerel, octopus, squid, swordfish, turbot, whale, crab, lobster, shrimp, oysters, scallops, prawn

Many people ask why the foods listed as unclean in the Bible are unhealthy to eat. There are many reasons these animals are unfit for human consumption. Take shellfish and pork as just two examples. Shellfish quite often have extremely high levels of toxic materials and parasites. Here in Florida, twenty people die each year from eating shellfish. We must remember that shellfish and other types of unclean fish are in the water for a purpose. They are scavengers! Their primary purpose in the food chain is to eat the debris and eliminated waste of other fish.

A lobster is an arthropod, and so is a cockroach. A lobster is a giant cockroach from the ocean floor. Enough said!

Pork does several bad things to the body. It causes a rapid rise in blood ureas. It digests too quickly. It causes the blood to get too thick and puts excessive stress on the cardiovascular system. It is loaded with fat.

Then there are the parasites. Approximately one out of three people in this country who are autopsied have trichinosis, which typically comes from eating tainted pork. Experiments have taken pork meat and heated it up to 600 degrees until the meat is totally charred and black. Under a microscope, some trichinae larvae are still alive! Do you really think you're going to cook the parasites until they are dead in your oven? Why would you want to eat cooked parasites anyway?

We once received a letter about pork from a custom meat butcher. The man had worked in meat cutting for many years as an inspector and had several people working for him. He had never seen a single pig cut open that wasn't filled with parasites and worms. It seems that certain animals are designed to have parasites living in them.

Unclean foods get eaten, but they're not healthy to eat. No wonder God warned us about unclean meat. A side note: I realize that as Christians we are not under the Old Testament Law, but to me, it makes sense to follow God's dietary guidelines as closely as possible.

Now that you've reviewed some of the problems and dangers of bad eating, it's time to cheer up a little! In the sections to come, I'm going to lead you into practical, step-by-step nutrition and menu-planning strategies for your child—at each stage of his development. We'll start right at the beginning, with prenatal nutrition.

# PART II:

## THE GOAL: A FAMILY OF HEALTHY EATERS

# 4

**✳✳✳✳✳✳✳**

# *Start With Baby…*
# *and Before*
### *(Prenatal Nutrition)*

Dear Future Moms and Dads,

It's possible to give birth to a perfectly healthy baby. A baby that will sleep through the night, never have diaper rash and experience very little problems with teething. This baby will have a great appetite and live in a family that doesn't pay huge pediatric medical bills. Sound good? I tell you, though, it's not easy, nor is it convenient all of the time. But taking the pains to prepare you for this child is well worth the joy it brings. I have always heard, "A happy baby is a healthy baby, and a healthy baby is a happy baby." That's our goal!

If you're planning to become pregnant, or you're already a mother-to-be, put aside any selfishness you have. No, you can't guarantee your child will have no congenital birth defects or diseases; bad things do happen to good people. But you can give that baby 100 percent when it comes to nutrition and love. So please don't put yourself first. Think of your baby's health and nutrition without compromise. The rewards will come.

## Preconception:  Prepare Yourself for Baby

The number one prerequisite for a healthy baby is healthy parents. Notice I said *parents*, plural. We aren't going to let your husband think that you, Mom, are the only one who's having this baby and that it all depends on what you eat. If you haven't conceived yet, then he is just as important in making that baby, and he needs to be concerned about his nutrition, too. Sometimes when a woman can't get pregnant, it's due to the husband's low sperm count. (By the way, we've had great results increasing sperm count with Prostality, Virility, zinc and vitamin E supplements: this subject is covered in depth in our Eat, Drink and Be Healthy program.) But even when everything's OK physically, the spiritual and psychological preparation for a new member of the family includes both parents. It ought to draw spouses very close and gear them up for a wonderful adventure in which they can share together.

### Preconception Nutrition

Most experts recommend that you start seriously watching your diet in terms of how it will affect your future child about six months before conception. Here are some quick and easy rules-of-thumb to follow:

- *Protein:* 50-70 milligrams per day—lean meats
- *Fiber:* 30 grams per day—fruits and vegetables
- *EPA:* 500 milligrams per day—cod liver oil
- *DHA:* 245 milligrams per day—essential fats

72

- *Iron:* 18 milligrams per day—unsulphured blackstrap molasses
- *Calcium:* 1,000 to 1,200 milligrams per day—green, leafy vegetables
- *Other nutrients:* usually 150 percent of the Recommended Daily Allowance (RDA) per day, paying special attention to zinc, magnesium, folic acid and vitamin D.

Eat "healthy" in general: low sugars, lots of vegetables, fruits and grains while avoiding red meats in favor of fish and poultry, low amounts of "processed foods," no junk foods, no caffeine, no alcohol and no smoking![1]

Naturally, though, we'll be focusing on the future mother's health and diet. If you can eat during the year before conception as though you were pregnant, you can increase the chances of having a healthy baby. A preconception diet is similar to a prenatal diet. The main difference has to do with fasting. In preconception, before you conceive your child, I suggest that both you and your husband fast one day a week. This will be a spiritual exercise that prepares your "inner environment" just as you are preparing the outer environment (by getting the nursery in shape). While you aren't eating, you can spend your time in prayer and meditation. Imagine and visualize all the ways you are going to love your baby. Place that child's life into the hands of God.

Most people can fast with no problems, but check with your doctor before you begin. Fasting should be well planned, of course. If you've never fasted or have a fear of fasting, start out by skipping just one meal during the week. During the next week, skip two meals in the same day. On the third week, try a thirty-six-hour fast by not eating three meals. If you are fasting one day a week, it's important to do so on the same day every week. The good Lord made our bodies to live by circadian rhythms.  After fasting on the same day for several weeks, your body won't want food on that day!

When fasting one day a week, drink plenty of distilled water.  If you are fasting more than one day, you may need some fruit juice added to your water.  If you feel you need more energy, sip on some unprocessed fruit juice or put a little honey under your tongue.  Fasting cleanses the body of toxic wastes and also helps return it to its ideal weight.

The biggest challenge most people have with fasting is breaking the fast properly.  Begin by doing so very slowly and with little food.  And remember: Rest is critical while fasting.  If you're used to a regular exercise program, you may want to lighten it a little bit.  Try to rest as much as possible.  Once you're pregnant, stop fasting!  That's the time when you want to be consuming all the essential nutrients your baby will need.

## *Care for Baby During Pregnancy*

The best possible diet for mothers-to-be consists of completely natural foods along with supplements.  A "back-to-nature diet" may be different from what you are used to, but remember that we are talking about supporting another life.  We want that support to be the healthiest it can be, which involves getting all the required nutrients while avoiding all the dangers of food processing.  Some of the most important things you need to be eating are protein, vegetables, fruits, grains, seeds, nuts, vitamins and minerals.  Let's look at these a little more closely, in whirlwind fashion.

## *The Womb/Placenta Connection*

The placenta is the main life support system of the fetus. Throughout the nine months of the baby's "space flight" in its

74

mother's womb, the placenta serves many complex functions for the developing fetus, including:

- Serving as a nutrition powerhouse transporting necessary fats, proteins, carbohydrates, vitamins, minerals and trace minerals
- Providing an efficient gas exchange of carbon dioxide and oxygen
- Working as a conduit of complex hormones, antibodies and enzymes
- Acting as a "filter" to refuse admittance to a number of organisms and chemicals that do the baby harm—items such as bacteria, viruses and other harmful infective organisms or environmental toxins
- Secreting hormones and other substances that support the pregnancy

The point is, the placenta itself needs much nutritional support from the mother.[2]

### *Pile on the Protein*

Most pregnant women have a protein deficiency. This is troubling, because many excellent sources of protein are available. You need about 75 grams of protein daily when you are pregnant and nursing, as opposed to 45 grams normally. Excellent sources of protein are goat's milk and raw cheese. Yes, you can eat raw cheese; just don't go to the store and buy the cheeses that are loaded with chemicals and artificial colorings. We know of a little vegetable market that sells raw, Amish-made cheese. They bring it down from Pennsylvania. It's raw cheese made with raw milk, loaded with calcium, and no yellow coloring. You can likely find something similar at your whole-food market.

However you get your protein, remember the baby comes first. Here's a reminder:

> Protein nutrition is important for both you and your baby. Inadequate protein can cause your body to lose lean muscle to supply the baby's needs because it's so important. However, if protein is seriously short, nature will not allow your health to deteriorate, because it plans for you to take care of the newborn baby. In that case, the baby suffers. All of this adds up to a simple dictum: Obtain sufficient protein. When in doubt, take out an inexpensive nutrition insurance policy in the form of a protein supplement.[3]

Beans and rice are excellent sources of protein. So are organic eggs. Clean fish are also good sources of protein. So when it comes to meat, eat a little bit of fish, a little bit of chicken and maybe a little bit of turkey. That's it. (When you're choosing chicken and turkey, look for a natural brand without hormones.)

I do suggest a protein supplement (such as this protein shake) when you're expecting. (We still drink this every day after we work out.)

### Protein Shake

2 cups water
1 scoop whey protein (made from organic milk)
1 Tbsp wheat bran
½ tsp unsulphured blackstrap molasses
½ Tbsp ascorbate vitamin C powder
1 tsp vanilla extract
1 Tbsp lecithin granules
2 frozen bananas
(peel ripe bananas, break into pieces and freeze)

1 handful frozen blueberries or raspberries
(or kids' favorite fruit)

Blend all ingredients together until smooth.

### *Eat Your Vegetables*

You need to eat as many raw or steamed vegetables as you possibly can. Try a fresh green salad every day or every other day. Get bib lettuce, endive or romaine lettuce. Use the dark green, leafy lettuce, and just make different salads. Put your favorite salad dressings on them, and you will start feeling really good. For variety, add chopped apples, grapes, currants (tiny raisins) or pine nuts.

### *My Favorite Salad*

You might like this, too: At our house we eat this salad at least twice a week. Use organic romaine lettuce and fresh spinach. Add a little shredded cabbage and half of a chopped apple; sprinkle pine nuts and currants on top. Add your favorite dressing. For protein, add either grilled chicken strips, cottage cheese or egg salad.

Buy your vegetables when they're in season. (If you have to use frozen vegetables for convenience, that's OK, occasionally.) My first choice is to get organically grown vegetables. Some co-ops have them available. They are going to be the best if you can get them. The next best way, would be to get them at your little roadside stand. The last place to get them would be at the grocery store. If you don't buy organic, be sure to wash vegetables with a biodegradable cleaner that will strip off many of the chemicals and sprays.

If you're going to be using beans, go with dried beans unless you get them fresh. You can buy organically grown beans at your health food store. They don't have any pesticides or herbicides, and the flavor is great. Soak them overnight and cook them in a little bit of unsulphured blackstrap molasses to help with iron uptake. They are great.

### *Feast on Fruits*

Have you noticed how hard it is to find sweet fruit today? The sweetness tells you about a fruit's nutritional value. The sweeter the fruit, the higher the mineral content. If the soil is low in minerals because of pesticides and herbicides (and because of a lack of good, old-fashioned crop rotation), the fruit won't be very nutritious. That's why we are going to talk about supplementing your diet with vitamins.

Fruit is very easily digested. Dried fruit is a good snack, but make sure it is unsulphured. It's always best to presoak it if you can. Frozen fruit can be used because fruit is such a seasonal item. I used a brand called *Cascadian Farms* that we find in whole-food markets. They don't use any sugar, yet the fruit is sweet. So if you use that, why not take the frozen fruit and make milkshakes with it—with goat's milk, a little bit of Stevia, an all natural, herbal sweetener and unsulphured blackstrap molasses?

I also take peeled, ripe bananas, break them up and freeze them. That's a great snack when you're pregnant. You can take these frozen bananas, run them through a juicer and have soft-serve banana ice cream. It's great!

### *Go With Grains, Seeds and Nuts*

Grains, seeds and nuts are excellent sources of protein, E vitamins and B vitamins. They are also the best natural source of unsaturated fatty acids, lecithin and trace minerals. Try buckwheat, millet and other fresh grains. Buckwheat pancakes are wonderful. Both Arrowhead Mills and Walnut Acres make a

78

great mix (call 1-800-434-4246 to order, or go to www.arrowheadmills.com).

Most people think seeds are bird food. Yet they're excellent for humans, very high in enzymes and trace minerals that we normally can't get in our diets elsewhere. They also are very high in manganese, an important nutrient for the reproductive system.

I have a recipe called Three-Seed Granola. You need a grinder, like a coffee grinder, to make it. Then you use flaxseeds, sesame seeds and sunflower seeds.

## Three-Seed Granola

Make sure you purchase seeds that have been refrigerated.

½ cup flaxseeds                    ½ cup sunflower seeds
½ cup sesame seeds                 ¼ cup brown rice syrup or
1/8 cup agave sweetener

In a small coffee grinder, grind each portion of seeds. Mix all together in a bowl. Stir in brown rice syrup until slightly sweet. Store in refrigerator and eat as a cereal.

One other thing: When you buy nuts, try to get them still in the shells. Otherwise, you'll need to refrigerate them, along with your seeds. (Seeds have a very high tendency to go rancid, so I suggest that you purchase them from a health food store that refrigerates them. If you go in a store and the seeds are out in the open in a grain bin, avoid them.)

### *A Good Idea: Supplement Your Diet*

Some people say, "Well, if I eat like you're saying, I'm not going to need any vitamins because I'll get everything I need from natural foods." Not so! When you're pregnant, your nutrient needs increase by two. Remember the baby?

## *Take Your Vitamins!*

My main point at the outset is this: Avoid taking synthetic chemical vitamins. If you go to the doctor, she'll prescribe a vitamin—and prescription vitamins are usually synthetic, often made from coal-tar derivatives. Those supplements don't feed the cells. You need a natural supplement that will feed the cells, give the cells life and put nutrients into those cells. Be very cautious. (You can order a complete line of vitamins and other supplements from our office; they can be shipped right to your home or business. Also, call our counseling line if you have questions concerning what you need: 1-800-726-1834 or www.healthmasters.com.)

## *Dangers of Vitamin Deficiency*

Supplementing during your pregnancy can make a big difference in the health of your baby, even to the extent of avoiding birth defects. According to Dr. Linda Rodriguez:

- Deficiencies in vitamin A and folic acid are known to cause birth defects such as cleft palate and neural tube defects, which affect brain and spinal cord.
- Iron deficiency and other anemia's may lead to smaller, anemic, sickly babies who may experience frequent illnesses along with growth and developmental delays.
- Calcium, magnesium and protein deficiency may be associated with toxemia of pregnancy, growth and mental retardation. This is especially true with a protein intake

of less than 45 grams a day during pregnancy. Aim for 90 grams of protein a day.[4]

Again, make sure your vitamins are natural. Don't go for the cheapest. Don't get your drug store specials here. If you buy the cheapest, you'll certainly get what you pay for: cheap nutrition. I'm just trying to stress the importance here of a good multivitamin that contains at least the pregnancy RDA. It shouldn't have sugars or fillers in it. It should be made from a natural food source.

> During your pregnancy, your nutrition requirement for most vitamins and minerals increases by 25 to 50 percent, and for some even more; for example, folic acid (100 percent increase) and iron (100 to 300 percent increase!), supplements are absolutely essential!
>
> Look at it this way: During normal non-pregnant times, 60 percent of all women fall 35 percent short of the RDA for calcium, magnesium, zinc, iron, folic acid, vitamins B6, B1, A, and D. If, during pregnancy and nursing, you must increase the intake of these nutrients by 100 to 300 percent, logic dictates that supplements are absolutely essential.[5]

Here are some of the critical vitamins you need for your baby's healthy growth in your womb. These can be purchased through our office at 1-800-726-1834 or through our website at www.healthmasters.com:

- *Cortico B*—This is a water-soluble B vitamin, which means that it's depleted on a daily basis. It goes in, and it's washed out. It's very important for your nervous and immune systems. There is some evidence showing that morning sickness stems from a shortage of folic acid, which is found in our prenatal vitamin. You need at least

800 micrograms per day. I suggest this before pregnancy and during pregnancy.

- *Ossomag (calcium, magnesium and vitamin D)*—You need a lot of calcium when you are pregnant, and it can be stored in your system. Consume about 800 milligrams daily. You need about 400 milligrams of magnesium and 200 International Units of vitamin D. Calcium maintains strong teeth and bones. (By the way, goat's milk is loaded with calcium.) Vitamin D helps your body to absorb the calcium. If you are a nursing mother, put calcium into your diet! I also suggest 2 tablespoons of cod liver oil, mixed with a little bit of juice. The brand I use is V.E. Irons. After you open it, keep it in the refrigerator.

- *E-400 w/Selenium*—Selenium works better with vitamin E than it does by itself. Vitamin E and selenium are needed to reduce the red blood cell formation.

- *Excellent C*—You need 1,000 to 1,500 milligrams a day of vitamin C. You can't overdose on it, because it is water-soluble. It's eliminated from the body, by the urine, the breath and perspiration on a daily basis. Vitamin C helps improve the immune system, and it also helps with resistance to disease. Stress will totally deplete your vitamin C levels. Birth control pills and smoking will deplete vitamin C as well. So take it on a daily basis.

### *Munch These Minerals!*

What is a mineral? It's a non-organic element that turns to ash when burned. Aren't you happy to know that? Around five dozen minerals exist, and twenty-two of them are necessary for good health. We've already mentioned your need for calcium during pregnancy, so I'll add the three other crucial minerals here:

- *Iron*—The simple fact is that your ordinary diet can't provide enough of this when you're pregnant. You need 30 to 60 milligrams during pregnancy, and the best natural source for iron is unsulphured blackstrap molasses. It isn't the best tasting stuff, but chase it with some juice. The end point of an iron deficiency is anemia, and you can't afford to be anemic when you're pregnant. When I make my protein shakes with the frozen fruit and a little bit of protein powder, I also put in one-half teaspoon blackstrap molasses, and I don't really taste it. There are ways to get it in your diet, but please do get it in your diet.
- *Zinc*—This is vital for tissue development. What does that tell about your baby? Zinc supports the immune system and the development of the brain and sexual organs. You need at least 25 milligrams of zinc daily. A zinc deficiency would cause poor and delayed wound healing as well. It has been shown in men to help increase the sperm count. So if you have not gotten pregnant, and you have been trying for a while, have your husband try that. A zinc deficiency may be evident when rapid cell growth is required (which happens in pregnancy).
- *Potassium*—At our house, we eat lots of bananas, which are an excellent source of potassium, in our protein shakes. (Note: As with vitamins, be sure not to overdose on any minerals. This could be dangerous to your health, so check with your doctor for the best dosages in your particular case.)

### *A Few More Important Things…*

Does it seem your "shopping list" is getting pretty long? Well, I just want to add a couple more things to help ensure your healthy pregnancy.

### The importance of fiber

"An apple a day keeps the doctor away." There's more truth to that ancient aphorism than you might think. Apples (and other fruits) are a good source of fiber, and consuming adequate fiber will keep your colon free of illness-producing "back ups." The fact is, a pregnant woman needs to have regular bowel movements. For one thing, the extra iron you may be taking in tablet form can cause constipation. The other problem is that you are going to be more prone to hemorrhoids and varicose veins during this time, you don't need to be straining to use the bathroom. To avoid consumption, increase your fiber intake. The main medical purpose for this is to keep cleaning out the colon. You see, when the colon gets sluggish and slow, toxins and poisons just sit there to be reabsorbed into the body. This also causes mucus buildup, especially in the lymphatic system. High-constipating foods include pizza, peanut butter, white bread and cheese.

Try to take in about 30 grams of fiber a day, which includes about 9 grams from a supplement, if necessary. But here's the key to making fiber work: Drink water.

### The importance of good water

Why is good water so important? It's the major detoxifier and purifier of the body. Drink half your body weight in ounces ever day. (Divide your pounds by two; that's how many ounces you need to drink on a daily basis.) The water will flush the system, keep the colon cleansed and keep the sugars and salts lower. In other words, we don't have to give up salt completely. We do need to refine it in our diet; moderation is the key. Salt in moderation is all right—if you know what moderation is. If you drink enough water, you can keep your salt levels almost perfect.

## *Tap Water and Artery Blockage*

We strongly believe quality water is the best treatment for all health disorders on our planet. The average amount of water in a human body is 65 percent, but it varies considerably from person to person, and even from one body part to another. The lowering of the water content in the blood triggers the *hypothalamus*, which is the brain's thirst center, to send out the demand for a drink.

As inorganic minerals, mainly from drinking tap water, enter the bloodstream, traces of these minerals adhere to the artery walls. Cholesterol sticks to them, causing the arteries to narrow, risking possible blockage. Other deposits from inorganic minerals occur where blood flow is slowest, including:

- Joints (can cause arthritis)
- Small veins (can cause varicose veins)
- Small arteries (can cause hardening)
- Inner ear (can cause hearing loss)
- Eye lens (can cause cataracts)
- Lungs (can cause emphysema)

My key concern is that you recognize how bad your tap water is, no matter where you live. It's invariably full of harmful chemicals and inorganic minerals that are useless to your body. In general, it's just not pure enough for human consumption. Consider just one link to a major disease: "Researchers have found that Parkinson's disease sufferers are more likely to have drunk well water and lived in rural areas than people without the disease. Risk of Parkinson's may be linked to an overload of environmental toxins. William Koller, M.D., a neurologist at the University of Kansas, believes toxins are the cause of this disease, but which toxins specifically are unknown."[7]

Giardiasis, which is caused by an intestinal parasite from drinking water, is on the rise. More than twenty thousand cases have been reported in the United States so far. And over the past few years, the EPA has cited water safety standard violations in more than one-third of all community water systems. We're talking about more than seven hundred contaminants in water supplies nationwide—and two hundred of them are toxic chemicals! The EPA only monitors thirty-eight chemicals.[8]

In spite of such facts, I had a personal experience with water that made even more of an impact on me. You see, we have a very good water system hooked up to our home's plumbing. First, the water goes through a reverse-osmosis fiber, then through a carbon filter and then that water feeds into our steam distiller. The final product is piped to our refrigerator, so we have good, clean water and ice. But the distiller has to be cleaned about every three months.

Once, when we were on the road a lot, we failed to clean that distiller for about five months. When my husband removed the canister holding the water being distilled, it was lined with inorganic mineral deposits. He soaked the canister in vinegar for twenty-four hours, and some of the hard, crust-like substance came loose. The rest he had to chisel off the sides. Here's the point: Remember that this water had already gone through two filters. And these inorganic materials are the same thing that contributes to hardening of the arteries!

I could go on and on about water, but can you see why I started adding steam-distilled water to my diet? I urge you to do the same. Why steam-distilled water? It's the same water your body manufactures; it's clean, with no salts or minerals.

86

## *Where Do You Find Steam-Distilled Water?*

We started buying our steam-distilled water at the grocery store in plastic one-gallon jugs. But one disadvantage of buying water in a thin plastic jug is that the water is poured into the jugs while it's still hot, which gives the water a plastic taste and allows toxins to leach out into the water.

When we could afford it, we had a local water company deliver five-gallon hard plastic jugs to our home with a water dispenser. Our final step was to purchase our own water distiller. We now have a fifteen-gallon tank that connects to a pump, which pumps water to our refrigerator door and to a gooseneck faucet at our kitchen sink. The water has a slightly sweet taste, and the convenience is wonderful.

If you can't start with a distiller, buy a good reverse-osmosis unit to get you started. We have both of these units available through our office, 1-800-726-1834.

## *The Importance of Exercise*

It's very important to be walking and getting yourself toned up before and during pregnancy. Many women say, "Well, I'm pregnant now, and I'm just going to let myself go until I have the baby. It's easier that way, and I can get away with it. No one can say anything to me."

This is not a good attitude. We need to try and keep our bodies in shape as much as we can. Just stay toned. I guarantee you that if you are toned during pregnancy, it is going to be a lot easier to get back into shape after you have your baby. Exercise also helps get oxygen to the cells and to the brain.

Try to exercise at least three to four times a week for thirty minutes. Find something that fits your schedule, even if its just for twenty minutes. What works best for many mothers-to-be is simply walking. I realize that some ladies could do high-impact aerobics and never affect their pregnancies. But it's better to be cautious and back off of the intensity until after the baby is born. Walking is the safest form of exercise while pregnant. Why not invest in some high-quality walking or cross-trainer shoes? Schedule it into your daily routine. (Note: Always check with your doctor before beginning any exercise program during pregnancy.)

## _The Importance of Essential Fatty Acids:  EPA and DHA_

The best way to keep your cholesterol levels healthy is to get enough essential fatty acids into your diet. EPA and DHA are two that you need. Both work in your blood vessels to reduce arterial plaque and to keep blood platelets from "clumping up." That's pretty important when it comes to preventing heart disease!

> Studies are now showing that children diagnosed with ADHD were deficient in essential fatty acids as infants. Remember that it is critical for the baby to receive adequate essential fatty acids during the first six months of life for proper brain and nerve development. Even after the baby is weaned, it's important to keep the child supplied with essential fatty acids.

For years, researchers have pointed to the fact that Eskimos, who eat lots of fish experience a very low incidence of heart attacks and strokes. (However, overdosing can cause problems with bruising, blood thinning and anemia. Be wise here!) You can get your essential fatty acids by eating oily fish, such as anchovies, sardines or salmon. Of course, I recommend salmon as the best source. Two other important oils for pregnancy are cod liver oil and flaxseed oil. Pregnant women in their last trimester should take one tablespoon, of each per day.

Even animals need their essential fatty acids to remain healthy. I saw this powerfully demonstrated in a zoo crisis that occurred with two sickly polar bears named Klondike and Snow. In the spring of 1996, my family visited the Denver Zoo to see the new twin baby polar bears. They'd been found almost frozen to death and rejected by their mother.

The nursery and veterinary staff had never faced such an incredible challenge. Never before had they raised newborn polar bears. Less than twenty-four hours old, they weighed in under a pound each! It took five hours in intensive care to get their body temperatures up to 100 degrees.

Over the next few weeks, it looked as though the cubs wouldn't make it through another day. Initially, the staff decided to tube-feed the babies, but they were stumped, not knowing what kind of formula to make for baby polar bears. It would take much guesswork and trial and error to keep the bears alive. The formula they decided upon consisted of puppy powdered milk formula: half-and-half, a vitamin and mineral supplement and safflower oil. (I would have used goat's milk. Plus, have you ever read the ingredients in half-and-half?)

Over a period of a few days, Klondike's health lagged behind; he quit gaining weight and started to bloat. The staff members thought they were going to lose him. Then Snow also began to fail and bloat. X-rays showed the bears' bone development was abnormal. Both babies' x-rays revealed many fractures, along with a case of rickets. Their bones were very brittle and unable to support any weight.

With more research, the staff decided to replace the safflower oil in the bears' formula with cod liver oil. After forty-eight hours, they began seeing dramatic improvements. One week later, the bears were x-rayed again, and good news! The fractures were already beginning to heal. I firmly believe the cod liver oil was the key to reversing the bone development problems in these baby bears. If that is the case, doesn't it make you more eager to take your own daily dose—and give it to your children?

As Klondike and Snow outgrew the nursery, another challenge arose. Where would these growing bears go for their permanent home? Denver Zoo didn't have a large enough facility to house two more bears. So guess where they ended up? They were flown to Sea World in Orlando—about a thirty-minute drive from my home. When we visited them recently, they seemed as happy and as healthy as could be. I watched them for almost an hour as they dove into the water and played with a large plastic garbage can. I thought, *How blessed my family is to see the miracle of these bears!*

God has made His creatures' bodies so resilient that if they are just provided with what they're lacking, in most cases, they will heal quickly. Remember, "Where there's slack, there's lack." Don't slack!

# 5

\*\*\*\*\*\*\*

# *Keep the Little Ones Eating Right*

## *(Infant and Toddler Nutrition)*

W E WERE SITTING in church one Sunday, but not in peace. In the pew behind us a little baby was screaming his lungs out. *What's wrong with this little guy?* I wondered.  As we started to move to a more eardrum-friendly part of the sanctuary, my husband leaned over toward the mother and asked, "What are you feeding your baby in that bottle?"  The mother replied without batting an eye, "Coke."

Needless to say, our mouths dropped open as I proceeded to pull on Ted's arm, hoping he wouldn't launch into our standard "Don't you know…" lecture.  He refrained.  But the incident really tugged at our hearts for the rest of the day, because that baby had no choice in planning his diet.  And he had good reason to cry.

I'm sure that you, as a conscientious parent, want to do the very best for your baby. From before day one, you start training your child in the way he should eat by caring for your baby. From before day one, you start training your child in the way he should eat by caring for your own preconception diet. Then, Mom, on day one you face a momentous decision.

### *To Nurse or Not to Nurse?*

That is the question. The answer is: Yes, nurse!

If you can do it, it's the best thing for your infant. Unless there is a good, medical reason not to nurse—a reason beyond your control—it's the best possible way to nourish your child during at least the first six months of life. In the 1940's and 1950's the "bottle revolution" broke out. Doctors and "modern" mothers felt that certain disadvantages attached to breastfeeding made it a problem: It was "inconvenient" or "time consuming." Are these really serious problems? Now let's consider the benefits for both mother and child. For example, the suckling of the newborn stimulates the release of a hormone that helps shrink the mother's uterus back to normal. For the baby, there are fewer colds, less colic and the development of a special emotional bond called *love*.

> Typical symptoms of colic include crying for up to two hours after feeding, writhing in agony and exhibiting a pale face with blue-grey just between the lips and nose. Your child may sweat from the scalp and have a lot of gas "at both ends." You may hear gurgling noises from the stomach.

> Colic is actually a vaguely defined condition, even among pediatricians. It usually begins after an initial "good" period of two to three weeks and seldom lasts longer than

three months. Nobody really knows the cause, but if you're having an ongoing problem, consider cutting back on any stressful aspects of the environment that your baby may be picking up on. Also check with your doctor to discover if there are overactive muscular movements in the colon, trapped gas in the lower bowel or a reaction to formula. If you are giving iron drops, that may be the cause. Or you may have started solid foods too early. Also check for allergies to foods, formulas or vitamins.

### *Start Out With Colostrum*

It all begins with colostrum, the thick, non-milk breast secretion formed in your mammary glands before your baby is born. It is the substance your baby eats during the first three days of nursing. And it is an absolutely wonderful food—the most important food your newborn infant will ever consume. It passes along your immunity toward certain diseases. It is higher in protein, vitamins and minerals than breast milk and lower in fat and milk sugar.

Colostrum contains substances that destroy viruses. It starts proper bowel movement in the newborn, furnishing the important acidophilus bacteria to the baby's bowels. Researchers have estimated that colostrum triggers at least fifty processes and functions in the newborn that provide lasting benefits!

Being a non-milk, colostrum is much higher in protein and has ten to seventeen times the iron content of milk, three times as much vitamin D and ten times more vitamin A.[1] Immunoglobulins, from which antibodies are formed, make up the majority of protein in colostrums.

Again, my first choice for a mother with a newborn is to breast-feed her baby. But I realize that sometimes a mother may have problems with her nipples or some type of other medical problem.  If you are adopting your baby, you may need some alternatives.  If you can't breast-feed, I have good news.  Research has found that colostrum from goats is much more potent than human colostrum.  The disease-resistant factors in the colostrum are simply transferred to the person (or animal) who uses it.  Goat colostrum can be processed, dried into a powder and is now being made available to the public.  Make sure the original source is from selected, pre-tested, disease-free, registered, grade-A dairy goats that have given birth to at least three kids.  Also ask about colostrum where you purchase your goat's milk; they may have some fresh or frozen available.

### *Cow's Milk Allergy Alert*

Studies show that as many as 7.5 percent of all babies born develop a hypersensitivity to cow's milk, generally known as Cow's Milk Allergy (CMA).  For a large number of adults, everyday problems relating to skin disorders, respiratory problems, gastric upsets and migraine are generally not considered to be related to cow's milk but are later diagnosed to be symptoms of CMA.

The most common symptoms evident in babies suffering from CMA are:

- Eczema
- Recurrent diarrhea
- Recurrent rhinorrhea
- Repeated vomiting
- Persistent colic
- Recurrent bronchitis
- Large mucus buildup and congestion
- Asthma

Evidence has shown that as many as 99 percent of all CMA sufferers are able to thrive on goat's milk.[2]

94

## *Use Breast Milk If You Possibly Can*

Breast milk really is superior to any artificial formula for your baby, and not only because of the colostrums benefit. Breast milk contains everything your infant needs, and it is more easily digested and assimilated than cow's milk. Nursing also prevents anemia in your baby while suppressing the instances of skin disorders in the child. There is also a decreased chance of infection and little, if any, constipation.

Your nursing baby will likely avoid allergies too. When a baby is born, his digestive system is still developing. A certain starch-digesting enzyme won't likely appear in his system until at least six months. Some babies are fed cereals four to six weeks after birth, but cereals are rich in starch. When you feed infants foods they can't digest, you can cause allergies. That's why healthy babies are usually nursed exclusively—with nothing else—for at least six months.

## *The Values of Breast Milk*

Here are some of the distinct advantages of feeding breast milk to your infant. Breast milk is:

- Non-allergenic
- Free of contaminating bacteria
- Easily digestible, producing small curds for easy absorption
- Rich in a factor that promotes the maturation of the gastrointestinal tract
- Filled with immunological factors such as bacterial and viral antibodies and a "growth factor" for the colonization by *lactobacillus bifidus*, an essential part of the immune defense system

95

- A source of a specific protein that can block the growth of *e coli* in the intestine, preventing diarrhea in infants
- Loaded with human brain growth factors
- Ideal in its calcium/phosphorus ratio for humans and low in sodium
- Important in maternal-infant bonding, providing nourishment of both body and soul
- Comes from a convenient, readily available source[3]

How long should you nurse? Everyone's circumstances vary, but if your milk supply is plentiful, it's best to nurse for at least one year to eighteen months. I know that is a long time, but it's a goal to train for.

I nursed our first son for nine months. I wanted to go for at least a year, but at that time we were in an expansion phase of our business. Our office was unbelievably hectic, and stress is one of the main things that cause milk to slow down. So the timing of nursing depends on what's happening in your life. The bottom line, though, is this: While you are nursing, be sure to drink at least eight to twelve glasses of distilled water a day, get plenty of sleep and maintain your high-nutrient diet.

If you're concerned your baby isn't getting enough breast milk, check out the following:

Is the baby's rate of weight gain OK? (You may have to check with your health care provider to find out. Few women have an infant scale at home.)

Are there fewer than six to eight wet diapers a day? Does the baby have fewer than three to five bowel movements daily? There should be at least this many.

Is the inside of the baby's mouth dry? It should be moist.

Can you hear the baby swallow milk while feeding? Swallowing noises should be audible.
Is the baby's suck weak? It should be strong, especially at the beginning of the feeding.

Is the duration of feeding short, or less than a few minutes? Babies usually consume 70 percent of the total milk within five minutes of beginning breast-feeding and 90 percent by ten minutes.

Is the frequency of feeding less than eight times a day? Babies are generally hungry eight to twelve times per day in the early months of life.

Are you experiencing the letdown reflex? Many women can feel the letdown reflex as a prickly sensation in the nipples within the first minute of breastfeeding. You know you have experienced the letdown reflex if milk spurts, rather than drips from your breast when the baby is removed a minute or so after breastfeeding has begun.[4]

## *Use Goat's Milk, Too*

During the months that you are nursing, I suggest giving your child no cow's milk at all. Cow's milk contains antibiotics and hormones, and many nutrients have been removed through pasteurizing and homogenizing. It causes a lot of children to have allergies and high levels of mucus formation. The high-heat processing destroys good enzymes in cow's milk, mainly phosphoritase, which helps the body absorb calcium. So if you go to cow's milk for the calcium, you should realize that not much actually makes it into your child's system.

If your baby is not staying satisfied, you can start supplementing with goat's milk. If you have had a stressful situation, and your milk slows up, you don't want a hungry baby! Do everything you possibly can, not to give them store-bought formula; you are just asking for troubles down the road. The only alternative I can suggest is goat's milk. We have seen miracle after miracle with raw, certified goat's milk. Besides your breast milk, goat's milk should be the only source of food for your child until he is about six to seven months old!

I can't say enough about the goodness of raw, certified goat's milk for your baby. For one thing, of all the goat farms I've either visited or called on the phone, I've found that very few of them got started because the owners said, "Oh, wouldn't it be fun to raise goats." No, they originally needed the milk for a family members' health problem. I find that very instructive. But listen to what Dr. Bernard Jensen, a leading nutrition expert, said:

> Over the fifty years of my work in the healing art, I have seen seemingly hopeless cases revived from the death bed with fresh, warm goat milk...[It] digests in twenty minutes, in comparison with cow milk, which takes two to three hours to digest. Goat milk is nutritionally balanced to nourish a kid weighing 6 to 10 pounds, about the same as the weight of a human baby. Cow milk is for a calf weighing 65 pounds at birth. The fat globules in cow milk are five times larger, which is why cow milk is much harder to digest than goat milk. It is also the reason why some babies get colic after drinking cow milk.[5]

Mom and Dad, you need to find a reliable source of raw goat's milk, no matter what it takes. When I say that it must be "raw" (state certified for cleanliness and bacteria count), I mean that it's not pasteurized or artificially homogenized (actually, goat's milk is already naturally homogenized). This kills the live enzymes that help the baby to digest the protein and the calcium in the milk. One live enzyme is fluorine, nature's fluoride. It builds hardness in bones and teeth.

Using goat's milk is so important that I want to give you step-by-step guidelines about it. Think of this as my "prescription" for your baby's health.

### *Find a good, reliable source.*

That's your challenge, and it is well worth the effort. Take these steps: First, go to your farm and garden center and ask for a list of people who buy goat feed from them. Next, go to those people; introduce yourself and tell them about your need. See if they have raw, certified goat's milk. You do not want it pasteurized; if it isn't raw, do not give it to your baby. Finally, arrange with these folks to obtain a regular supply.

Even if you live in the city, finding raw goat's milk shouldn't be too difficult. Try leaving the city and driving to the closest rural town. In the phone book, look up the largest farm and garden center listed in that area and proceed with the second step above.

### *Mix your formula.*

Goat's milk is high in calories, and it will satisfy the baby. You'll find the formula I suggest within the chart below. Notice that it varies a bit, depending on the age of your child.

### *The Ultimate Goat's Milk Formula*

Day 1 to Day 3
Colostrum (if not available where you purchase your goat's milk, mix 1 ounce goat's milk and 1 ounce distilled water with 3 to 4 capsules of powdered colostrum)

Day 4 to Day 7
2 parts raw goat's milk, 1 part colostrum, 1 part distilled water

For infants older than one week, add the following ingredients to one gallon of goat's milk and shake well. Then pour the formula into bottles for your baby.

If your baby is staying hungry, decrease water slowly but if your baby gets constipated, you may need to add extra water. Every baby is different.

1 week to 3 months
½ tsp blackstrap molasses (unsulphured)
Contents of 1 capsule folic acid (800 mcg)
Contents of 1 capsule vitamin E (400 I.U. capsules, mixed tocopherols)
1/16 tsp vitamin C powder (powdered ascorbate 2,000 mg per tsp.)

Add to first and last bottle daily after bottle is warmed:
Flaxseed oil—5 drops
Cod liver oil—5 drops

3 months to 5 months
Increase:
Vitamin C to ¼ tsp*
Flaxseed oil to 10 drops
Cod liver oil to 10 drops

5 months
Add ½ oz. fresh carrot juice to each bottle (this prepares the baby's system for pureed food in the sixth month)

6 months to 12 months
Twice a day add the following oils *only after* the bottle is warmed:
Cod liver oil—1 tsp
Flaxseed oil—1 tsp

Increase vitamin C to ½ tsp and blackstrap molasses to 1 tsp per gallon of milk.

*Note: If baby's stool becomes runny, cut back on vitamin C. If stool is still runny, cut back on cod liver oil.

- Cod liver oil is one of the best natural sources of vitamin D for your baby. Vitamin D is what helps the body absorb calcium. Remember that this is oil, and it needs to be stored in the refrigerator after it's opened. I use the V.E. Irons brand. It is excellent, and we haven't had any problems with it. The kids get used to it.
- Blackstrap molasses prevents iron deficiency. Watch to see if the baby gets a little bit of a red bottom or rash because it is too strong for him at this time. Some babies are ready for it at six months, and some aren't. So you look at what I call baby's "nutritional barometer"—his little bottom. If it is starting to turn red, then cut back on the blackstrap molasses.
- Watch the water. Newborn infants very rarely need any extra water as long as the mother is drinking plenty of water. The first three months of mother's milk should be the total supply of nutrition and food. As they get older and are more active, you can start infants on about an ounce of distilled water a day. You can give it to them by the spoonful, and they will drink it. Water needs to be added to milk during the first three months.
- Freeze the goat's milk. If you can obtain a large supply of goat's milk, you can freeze it for up to six months. If you are buying it by the gallon and freezing it, thaw it out a gallon at a time. One gallon of milk may last you a week, but remember it has nothing in it to keep it from spoiling. It is raw nutrition, so it isn't going to last as long as other milks from the store. If you are not going through it very quickly, do freeze your goat's milk.

Now, before leaving the subject of goat's milk, I want to offer one more item from Dr. Jensen about this wonderful food for your baby:

Some years ago, the *Journal of the American Medical Association* published an article titled "Dietetics and Hygiene," which reported: "The goat is the healthiest domestic animal known. Goat milk is superior in every respect to cow's milk. Goat milk is the ideal food for babies, convalescents and invalids, especially those with weakened digestive powers. Goat milk is the purest, most healthful and most complete food known."[6]

## *Introduction of Solid Foods*

6 months
The food is here! Slowly introduce solid foods: one bite of pureed banana mixed with goat's milk and one prepared formula bottle each feeding. Feed only pureed banana with bottle for about a week. Then gradually add more bananas to each. After several weeks, try another fruit.

Use only homemade or organic baby food: Try Earth's Best or Organic Baby (name brands); these are high quality and are found in health food stores and some grocery stores.

NOTE: The most important thing to remember is to introduce anything new, very slowly. Watch for any rashes, changes in bowel movements and so forth.

7 months to 8 months
Start introducing more organic fruits and vegetables; use baby food plus goat's milk formula.

12 months to 18 months
Start adding cereal.

1 year to 2 years
Feed with organic or homemade baby food plus goat's milk formula (in a sipper cup) daily. Remember that baby is still

growing and developing, outwardly and inwardly. Do not feed a baby adult food. His digestive system is not prepared and mature enough to assimilate and digest adult food properly.

## *Starting Juices and Solid Foods*

"When do I start my baby on solid foods?" All nursing mothers want to know the answer to this question. The answer has to do with your infant's maturity, her growing need for supplemental calories and her mastery of the swallowing reflex. Seek medical advice before starting solid foods, but realize that many young mothers do start too soon. Then they end up with a child who's suffering with digestive disturbances like constipation, gas, diarrhea and allergies.

Think about this. Let's say you went on a forty-day fast. (This is just an analogy remember!) Let's say on day forty-one you are going to eat. Now what are you going to put in your stomach? Not a major meal! You'd need to start out very slowly, very gradually, and treat that stomach as though it had never had food in it before. That's just how you'll treat your baby, as she starts moving to solid foods.

When they are about six to seven months, you can start infants with a little bit of diluted juice (such as fresh pear, grape, papaya, pineapple or apple). I suggest withholding any other juices until they're at least two years old. Pear and grape are very mild, not acid-forming and are easy on the system.

Here are my specific suggestions for various ages:

- *At six to seven months,* you can give a half-ounce to one-ounce portion of juice, two times a day. Cut the juice by ½ with distilled water. That is just enough to prepare their little systems to receive something "new" without causing a reaction. Again, watch their bottoms. When

103

introducing new foods you need to allow five days to one week on each new food, giving the baby's system time to get used to it. I personally don't like giving children juices since they are so concentrated with fruit sugar and can lead to a sweet tooth for other sweet drinks like soda.

After you've started on juice, mash up a very ripe banana and mix it with a small amount of goat's milk (or mash up a papaya). Make the mixture really watery so that there's not much fruit in it; however, you'll be giving them a little bit of substance for their stomach to work at digesting.

- *At nine months,* you can start them on a little bit of raw yogurt. Again, mix that with some raw goat's milk. Raw yogurt has the three living bacteria in it that are called "friendly bacteria" for the colon. This will help your baby get the digestive system started. Keifer may be introduced; this is great for the colon and bones. At this age, introduce fresh lemonade: 8 ounces distilled water, the juice of 2 fresh squeezed lemons, 6-12 drops of Stevia (or sweeten to taste).

As the digestive system develops, it is ready for more of an assortment of pureed vegetables and less water. In other words, if you start infants at nine months or so on some pureed vegetables and maybe some pureed fruit, you want to mix it with water or goat's milk and make it a little watery. But then, as they get older, you can start cutting back on the liquid and feeding more of a solid form.

Another good idea that works well with babies, is brewer's yeast. You can use about a quarter of a teaspoon in juice or mashed fruit. This is an excellent source of B vitamins for your child.

## *Starting Creamed Cereals*

So you're coming to the end of nursing your child, and the doctors says, "OK, now you can go ahead and start her on cereal." What do you do?

My idea of cereal is not going to the grocery store and buying those brand-name boxes or jars. My idea of cereal is taking brown-rice cereal that's organically grown, and cooking it. It is excellent, and baby doesn't even have to chew it! Brown rice is very, very high in nutrients.

We were doing some missionary work in Costa Rica, and we saw the people there eating tons of this rice—not the processed rice. And those folks were thriving on it! You see, brown rice still has the bran layer on it, and all the nutrients are intact. When it's ground, with a little sweetener or a little milk on it, it's great for weaning your children.

At twelve to eighteen months you can start your child on creamed cereals. I know that some children start on cereals at three weeks of age, and some start at three months of age. But remember the possible drawbacks to that. I suggest waiting until twelve to eighteen months. It has to do with waiting for that starch-digesting enzyme to fully mature in your child's digestive system. As I've mentioned, if that enzyme isn't fully present, the starches you're giving the baby can cause allergies and other problems.

When you are working with grains, why not get one of the little mini-grinders, an equivalent to a coffee grinder? (If it grinds coffee beans, it will grind grain.) Buy your grains fresh from a health food store. You can get millet, barley, buckwheat, wheat, oats and much more. I grind up about a cup at a time, and that allows it to stay fresh. Otherwise, they'll go rancid quickly unless refrigerated. Grind them into a flour consistency, out of which you'll make your cereal. (You need to keep those in the freezer because they will go rancid in twenty-four hours otherwise.)

To save time, you can make up a two-week's supply of creamed cereal. Use four containers, and put them in the freezer. I use brown rice as an excellent base for all the cereals. You can make cream of rice, cream of wheat, cream of buckwheat, cream of barley and so on. For instance, if you were going to make cream of wheat, mix together one cup of ground brown rice and one cup of ground whole wheat. Mix those together in a jar, and you have cream of wheat. You can take out a couple of tablespoons, mix it with some water and cook it on the stove.

### *Helpful Hints for Cooking Hot Cereals*

- Always add ground grains to water while the water is cold. If you add to boiling water, the cereal will be very lumpy.
- Most grains cook up well by using a 1 to 4 ratio (example: ¼ cup grains to 1 cup water). If grains are too thick, just add more water.
- Always bring cereal to a boil. It may have a thinner texture until it cools. The longer it cools, the thicker it gets.
- Remember, babies are not born with a "sweet tooth." Don't think you have to sweeten your baby's cereal to "your taste." At this age they start developing their taste habits. Why make them want sugar when they don't know the difference? (Also, do not potty-train a child with candy.)
- When adding any sweetener, start with the least sweet as your first choice. (Least sweet: Stevia, barley malt syrup, brown rice syrup, sorghum molasses, Agave Nectar. Sweetest: honey.)

Remember: When you start cereals, start them one at a time. Give infants about a week to get used to a particular cereal, observe their bodily reactions and then start them on another cereal. All of this is simply to make sure their systems can handle the changes.

When you're cooking the cereals, you usually want to use a one-to-four ratio. For instance, use ¼ cup of grains to one cup of water. If you're using barley and millet, these two grains require more water.

### *Honey Could Hurt Baby!*

Don't give honey to children under one year old. Their systems can't handle it, nor can their digestive tracts stop the growth of botulism spores sometimes found in certain honeys. These can be fatal to your infant!

*One other note:* When you make pureed foods for your child—for instance, vegetables or any of the leftovers you had the night before—just put them in the blender and add a little distilled water. Save some baby food jars, and put food in them. I cook a little bit of brown rice and use that as a base if I am making baby food this way. I cook the brown rice, and then I cook some other vegetables. After that, I mix them in the blender. The rice lends a thickness to keep everything from being too runny.

The point is, if you have the time, or if you have fruit and vegetables left over from your family meal, I suggest you make your own baby food as often as possible. Also, you can purchase a baby food grinder and instantly puree your baby's food at the table. Usually at two years old, children have at least four molars. At that time you can start adding a little finely chopped apple cooked into their creamed cereals. Or add some coconut or dried fruit, because they are now able to chew it. But don't push them; if they don't have the teeth to chew, then the food is going to go through them.

## *Baby Food Grinders*

One thing that has really helped me out is a little baby food grinder. The brand name is Happy Baby Food Grinder. They run about $18.00. You can buy them in the health food store, and they are so convenient. They are just made of plastic, and you can take them to the restaurant if you have vegetables to grind into baby food. You can also take it on trips. You can take it when you go to see relatives or spend the night somewhere. When we have leftovers—something that is too small to put in the blender—I just grind it up, put it in a bowl and my baby has a meal.

## *Offering Organic*

I know, store-bought baby food in jars is so convenient. It is so easy. But we are blessed today to have available to us several companies that manufacture organic baby food. A current Nielsen survey showed organic baby foods are the fastest-growing baby segment, up 400 percent nationally in the past twelve months. When it comes to saving money in your family budget, don't cut corners on baby food. Your baby is worth the best. Cut back on other items, but buy the best for your baby.

The availability of organic baby food has made it much more convenient for mothers who want the purest and most nutritious food possible. The preparation time alone is an incredible bonus. I personally prefer Earth's Best brand. They were the first in the industry to introduce organic baby food. Now other companies have followed in their footsteps, realizing the demand for pesticide and chemical-fee nutrition. Other brands include Organic Baby, and now even Gerber has awakened to the need with their Healthy Harvest line. By the way, it's also possible to buy organic baby food by mail order.

### *Finding Protein Replacements*

Children need a good source of protein every day. Here's a possible scenario for making sure this requirement is met:

- *First 2 years*: goat's milk, goat milk yogurt
- *Age 3*: goat's milk, raw cow's milk, organic eggs from this point forward, Keifer
- *Ages 4*-6: goat's milk (only if child does not have a weight problem or is not lactose-intolerant), raw cow's milk, organic eggs, protein shakes
- *Ages 7*-8: high-quality or fresh almond butter, protein shakes, organic eggs, cashews and almonds
- *Ages 8-12*: clean fish or high-quality organic chicken, protein shakes, organic eggs
- *Ages 12 and up*: high-quality beef (no more than once a week), protein shakes (plus the above)

At a young age, meat is not the answer. Animal protein is very difficult to digest, so if you can avoid beef altogether, that will be best for your family. Even adults that have no digestive problems cannot properly digest and assimilate animal protein properly. Our answer has always been "protein shakes" (recipe on page 76).

With protein shakes, find out what fruits your children especially like, and experiment with them until they begin asking you for the shake. Start with a high-quality whey protein powder. (Be careful; there are some really bad ones on the market, even sweetened with aspartame. We use just pure whey protein.) Start your child off slowly with the ingredients so she'll learn to like them. Choose her favorite natural extract and frozen fruit.

This shake has such a high-nutrient density that it would be great to start the day with it. Toddlers love it. Our oldest son has been drinking protein shakes since he started on solid foods. We now make up enough for all of us to have after we work out in the gym. Won't you join us?

## *Supplementing Your Child's Diet*

Why supplements? Today supplementation is a necessity. We are eating more and more processed foods and less and less fresh fruits, vegetables and grains. Our soils are depleted of essential vitamins and minerals, which in turn are lacking in our food. Today we take in more and more pollutants than ever before. It's not the way it was a hundred years ago on great-great-great-grandma's and grandpa's farm.

*Children need. . .*
- Vitamins
- Minerals
- Protein
- Carbohydrates
- Fat

*Vitamins, minerals, protein and fats for infants/toddlers*
- Goat's milk, mother's milk (raw cow's milk after age 2)
- Cod liver oil
- Flaxseed oil
- Liquid or powdered multiple vitamin
- Powdered vitamin C

*Vitamins, minerals, protein and fats for preschool children*
- Cod liver oil—2 tablespoons per day
- Flaxseed oil—2 teaspoons per day
- 500 milligrams extra vitamin C powder twice a day
- Multiple vitamin once a day

110

- ½ tsp unsulphured blackstrap molasses two times per week (best natural source of iron; can be put in a protein shake)

*Extras if needed (Substances marked with * are known as "cold busters")*

- B-complex (only take in the morning since it will increase energy levels)
- B6 (affects both physical and mental health; aids in the absorption of vitamin B12 in immune system function)
- B5 ("anti-stress vitamin"—pantothenic acid—helps in the production of the adrenal hormones and the formation of antibodies)
- *Zinc (promotes healthy immune system and healing of wounds; important in prostate gland function and the growth of the reproductive organs)
- *Pycnogenol (pine bark extract; a unique flavonol that clinical tests suggest may be as much as fifty times more potent than vitamin E and twenty times more potent than vitamin C in terms of antioxidant activity)
- Calcium (vital for the formation of strong bones and teeth; tends to have a calming effect on the body; best taken at night for its relaxation qualities)
- Alfalfa tablets (one of the most mineral-rich foods known to man; roots of the alfalfa plant grow as deep as 130 feet, picking up essential minerals)
- *Echinacea (stimulates certain white blood cells; good for immune system and lymphatic system)
- *Garlic capsules (or liquid; detoxifies the body and enhances immune system, which protects against infection)
- Wheat bran (extra fiber; used in recipes, cereal and protein shake, for example)

- Unsulphured blackstrap molasses (best natural source of iron)
- Aloe Vera juice (98-99 percent pure Aloe Vera juice, mixed with 1/3 cup fruit juice, helps aid in healing of stomach disorders and colon problems; helps alkalinize an acid system.  In general, try to feed your children more alkaline foods and less acidic foods.  The foods that are acidic cause the body itself to become acidic, which hinders proper food digestion.)

A special note about vitamin C:  Make sure that you are getting plenty of vitamin C in the first three to six months because, if your child is using you for the only source of food, that is how he is going to get his vitamin C.  Obtain an excellent source of ascorbate-powdered vitamin C.

I put powdered vitamin C in our children's goat milk and they get it every day.  The fact is they have very few colds.  But if I notice any type of cold symptoms beginning, I give them extra vitamin C to build their resistance levels.  (If resistance is low from lack of sleep or poor diet, then children are going to be more susceptible to colds.)

You also need to be consuming a high quality multiple vitamin when you nurse.  Make sure it's an excellent multiple vitamin— not a synthetic one that costs you $2.99 at the drug store.  You need to be getting a good multiple vitamin daily.

Choosing the right supplements can be very confusing if you don't know what to look for.  Remember:

- Make sure they come from a reputable source (call our office for information: 800-726-1834 or www.healthmasters.com).

- Children can swallow vitamins sooner than you think. My oldest son started at age two. He saw his father do it, so they made it a game. He wanted to copy my husband.
- Don't give your child and option. It's just like brushing teeth; do you let them have an option on that?

## Toddler Sample Menu

Breakfast:  Non-instant oatmeal with chopped apple cooked in, cool with milk (When cooking rolled oats, try replacing water with coconut milk; add shredded coconut and vanilla or chopped pears or raisins).
Snack:  Banana
Lunch:  Steamed (soft) broccoli with grated cheese on top, piece of whole-wheat toast
Snack:  Apple slices
Dinner:  Baked sweet potatoes, creamed spinach, glass of goat's milk

## Preschooler Sample Menu

Breakfast:  Hole-in-One (Cut hole out of a piece of whole-grain buttered toast.  Lay toast over one over-easy egg.  Place the "hole" on the plate.)
Snack:  Fresh fruit in season
Lunch:  Funny Face Sandwich (see section ten)
Snack:  Grapes, fresh or frozen
Dinner:  Broccoli or spinach quiche, pita crisp

# 6

**✳✳✳✳✳✳✳**

# *Fuel Those Active Minds and Bodies!*
## *(Children's Nutrition)*

I HAD A DEAR friend whose little girl was rushed to the hospital. This mom called me late one night and tearfully shared, "We just took Andrea to the emergency room. She has terrible abdominal pain, and we didn't know what to do. They've just completed some tests, and you know what? The doctor says it's her liver."

"What do they plan to do?" I asked.

"Well the doctor said that they're going to keep her here for a few days and put her on a non-meat diet."

Those "few days" made all the difference for Andrea. Within days we all discovered that the child's liver was significantly inflamed and swollen, at the age of two years old.  Red meat was named as the main culprit.

Within about a month Andrea's liver had returned to normal. And all the other problems associated with that panicky dash to the hospital disappeared.  You see, Andrea's liver couldn't produce the proper enzymes for her stomach to digest the meat. So there it sat in her colon, literally rotting inside of her until she passed it through.

Over the years we've seen this problem often:  Children are being fed foods that their little bodies aren't ready to digest. Just as a child is growing in stature and not fully matured on the outside, her digestive system hasn't fully developed on the inside.  We tend to recognize that she's a little child at a glance—after all, she only reaches our kneecaps.  Yet we may think her insides are mature, as if she were a little adult when it comes to nutritional processes.  How wrong we are!

Parents, it is our responsibility to shield and protect our children from any foods that can harm them—whether because the foods themselves are bad or because the child's digestive tract isn't ready.  The first form of protection requires constant monitoring of the "bad stuff" they tend to eat and replacing it with the "good stuff."  That's what we'll focus on in this section.

### _Replace the "Bad Stuff" for Your Kids!_

Where do we start when we decide to give up the bad stuff?  I'd suggest tackling the "big three white poisons" right at the start. You're better off staying away from them yourself, of course. But you sure don't want to give them to your kids.

## *Don't Administer These "Poisons"!*

We've all heard about these three "killers"—white sugar, white flour, white salt. I'm talking about those highly refined and processed varieties with very low—if any—nutritional value. They're as American as apple pie (and very much in the pie), but they've got to go.

"OK," you say. "You're telling me what to eliminate. Now what do I do about replacing these things?" As a matter of fact, I've got some great replacements for these three, and I'll also include in my list a number of other things to replace.

### *Replacing sugar*
A woman came up to me a while back with a look of shocked amazement. She said she'd gone into a health food store, and the shelves were displaying the number-one soft drink in America (it contains about ten teaspoons of sugar in a twelve-ounce bottle). I told her not be to so shocked. We'll never get away from our society's bent toward overloading with refined sugar. It's going to be with us—even when we walk into what ought to be "food heaven."

But we can walk past those shelves to the ones displaying better options. As far as sugar goes, a lot of people go from white sugar to honey. I'd caution you here, because honey is still very concentrated and has the highest sugar content of all natural sweeteners. It also has a higher calorie count than refined sugar. As a matter of fact, I was addicted to sugar; I like people to know that so they realize that I've "been there, done that." I went through this addiction with great difficulty. Then I thought that because I was eliminating white sugar and eating honey I had solved my sugar problem. But honey not eaten in moderation, can cause the same problems that sugar does.

Consumers are also being fooled by honey because there are good and bad varieties on the shelves. If it is heated to high temperatures to make it clear and apparently "pure," it's left virtually without nutrients. On the other hand, truly natural honey that is heated only to low temperatures contains natural enzymes and pollen, which supply rich protein. The other benefit of good honey is that it supplies small amounts of potassium, phosphorus and calcium.

There are other natural sweeteners for you to try, such as sorghum, date sugar, brown rice syrup, maple syrup, Stevia and Agave Nectar. Not many people are familiar with brown rice syrup, but I highly recommend it for its delivery of a delicious, sweet flavor without causing the body's sugar levels to rise very high. In fact, I use brown rice syrup, Agave Nectar and Stevia regularly as sugar substitutes. Remember that we need minerals in our diet, and refined white sugar has zero nutrients.

My point here is that your child should have very little white sugar in his diet. It's so much better to follow that simple rule. Today, many parents allow their children to eat sugar without any restriction at all. I find that very hard to understand. Many teens consume up to four hundred pounds of sugar per year! Fifty percent of a typical teenagers' daily intake in calories is sugar. That is really too high. No wonder they're so hyper.

The problem is that white sugar enlarges the kidneys and liver. It robs calcium from the body. It depletes B and C vitamins. It robs the body of other nutrients. It is rapidly absorbed into the blood system, which causes hyperactivity in a lot of kids. It is a cheap filler. (That's the main reason sugar is used.) It's in everything from fruit drinks, to canned soups, to ice cream, to mayonnaise, to pickles, to ketchup, to cereal, to soft drinks, and it goes on and on and on. But as prevalent as it is, it will keep letting you down.

## *The Big Letdown*

That instant pickup from a candy bar is really a downer in disguise. Why? Simple sugars, which most candies are, require little metabolizing and enter your bloodstream quickly, giving you that much-touted lift. But the catch is that your pancreas, the organ in charge of releasing insulin to process carbohydrates (starches and sugars) to keep blood sugar at a steady and healthy level, is caught off guard by the sudden surge of sugar and, thinking it has more work to do than it has, releases too much insulin. The result is an in-body processing error that lets you down the hard way: a drop in blood sugar, usually within the hour, that leaves you feeling less energetic, less alert and more hungry and irritable than you were before.[1]

Consider some of the alternatives. Ripe bananas, for instance, make a wonderful sweetener. You can use bananas to sweeten a lot of things. For example, you can make a real quick ice cream with frozen bananas, frozen fruit, a little bit of sweetener and all kinds of things in your blender. Just blend it until it is thick. This makes an excellent ice cream. Also, if you have an ice cream maker, why not just make your kids homemade ice cream?

Another good sweetener is barley malt syrup. It's not as sweet as other alternatives, but the flavor is really good. Then there's "nature's sweetener," Stevia. Have you heard of this remarkable herb that originally came from the mountains of Brazil and Paraguay? Sometimes called sweet herb, or honey leaf, this calorie-free wonder is fifty to four hundred times sweeter than sugar, is safe for diabetics and—unlike aspartame—can be used in baking. Unfortunately, it has been limited by the FDA to be sold only as a dietary supplement, though it's been used as a sweetener for hundreds of years in some cultures. If you'd like to find out more, write for the booklet produced by Woodland Publishing.[2]

Now, the big question about these sugar replacements is, Can you find them at your regular supermarket? The answer is, maybe…sometimes. Probably a specialty store or health food store is your best bet. A lot of the traditional grocery stores are starting to carry these sugar replacements now, but you have to be very careful because many of the varieties are highly processed. You can order the Stevia, agave nectar and brown rice syrup from our office at 1-800-726-1834.

### Replacing white flour
That favorite kind of bread all the neighbor kids are eating is, of course, white bread. But don't let your children touch it! It's made from highly processed, bleached and denitrified flour. It gets all that gooey softness from monoglycerides and diglycerides. And it is woefully lacking in fiber.

A child shouldn't be eating any white bread at all. I don't know how many of you remember "the good old days." My father told me that when he was in school they used to make their own glue. Know how they did it? They just mixed up some water and white, refined flour. You see, when white bread is made, the flour is milled into a fine powder. That destroys a lot of the nutrients right off the bat, but then it is bleached. After that, before the refined, bleached flour is actually made into bread (or "paste"?), a few vitamin tablets are thrown in. The bread is then called "enriched." Not a whole lot of nutrition here!

We knew of one little boy who had a "dough ball" in his colon the size of a tennis ball. He couldn't go to the bathroom. He was getting fuller and fuller. When we asked his mother what he was eating, she said, "Just pizza and peanut butter and jelly sandwiches made with white bread." He was in trouble! You see, the rhythmic action of the colon "kneads" the dough into dough balls, which may cause a "road block" in the intestinal tract. If the body doesn't eliminate on a regular basis (at least two times per day), many of the toxins are reabsorbed back

119

through the colon wall, causing autointoxication. A toxic body is not a healthy body; it opens the door for disease to set in.

I suggest no white bread for human consumption. Use it as paste for your homework projects only!

We usually go with Ezekiel bread. Available in most health food stores and also in the organic section of most grocery stores, it's made from sprouted grains, has a lot of fiber and abounds with nutrients. It is really good. Our children eat it as a snack.

Of course, you can make your own bread. I am not a bread maker. As a matter of fact, my sweet husband bought a bread machine, and I was kind of kidding our neighbors one day, saying, "I wake up in the morning to fresh, baked bread, and my husband makes it."

They said, "Where did you find this guy?"

I said, "He bought me a bread maker, and I have never learned to use it. So he makes it the night before, and it's ready in the morning."

But we don't make it that often. If we use bread, it's usually whole-wheat pita bread. There is whole-wheat pita bread in the grocery store, but it does have sugar in it, so be careful about what kind you get.

In spite of all that I've been telling you about white bread, some parents sill believe that enriched white bread is just as nutritious as whole wheat, because nutrients have been added back in after the milling and bleaching processes are complete. However, the bleaching is something you definitely want to avoid. These flours have been chemically whitened with benzoyl peroxide, chlorine dioxide or acetone peroxide. Sound appetizing?

Though the FDA says these chemicals are safe, consumer activists are constantly calling for further testing.

The most distressing thing about white bread is that some brands claim to have "no preservatives" on the label. Yet they usually have dough conditioners such as potassium bromate (hard on the central nervous system and kidneys) and sodium stearoyl lactylate. Then there's ammonium sulfate. Would you believe that is used in fireproofing your fabrics?

When you do use flour, I suggest you use whole-wheat flour. A lot of women like to use white flour as a thickener for gravies, starches and other sauces when they cook. I suggest you use arrowroot or rice flour instead. But remember: Whole-wheat flour goes rancid twenty-four to forty-eight hours after it's ground. Store it in the freezer.

### *Good Bread?*

We often choose "wheat" bread over "white" bread, assuming that the darker loaf is the healthier one. This is true only when the wheat is whole wheat. White bread is also made from wheat, and loaves that are marked "wheat" but not "whole wheat" are darker simply because caramel coloring has been added in the processing.[3]

Other good alternatives to white flour include whole-wheat pastry flour, oat flour, rice, rye or unbleached white flour when needed (depending on the recipes you use). For pasta and spaghetti made from white flour, try substituting with artichoke, spinach or corn pasta (found in health food stores). Good breads from your whole food market include Ezekiel bread and Tree of Life Seven-Grain bread.

**To thicken your sauces, try these substitutes:**
Original ingredient: 1-tablespoon all-purpose white flour

Substitutes: 1 ½ teaspoons aluminum-free cornstarch; 1 ½ teaspoons arrowroot; 1 tablespoon tapioca; 2 ½ teaspoons whole-grain flours; 1 tablespoon oat flour[4]

### *Replacing salt*
As far as using white salt, sea salt is a little better, but you've got to be careful because it's very concentrated. Another way to replace salt is to go with garlic powder, onion powder or other powdered herbs with strong flavor. There are loads of such seasonings on the market today.

It's estimated that we consume about fifteen pounds of salt per year. We like it, but it's a killer! Here are just a few of the problems it can create in our bodies: hypertension, potassium loss, fluid retention—and an increased risk of heart disease. The key to using salt: If you drink enough purified water daily, salt should not be a problem.

## *Drop That Steak, Mister!*

On the television show *20/20* several years back, Geraldo Rivera gave a special report about two-year-old Puerto Rican children who were eating a lot of meat, particularly beef and chicken. These little kids were developing breasts the size of full-grown women, sprouting pubic hair and experiencing unusual hormone changes. Researchers found out that these strange symptoms may have come from the kids' meat intake. The brands they were eating were loaded with chemicals and hormones—and it was showing up in the children's bra sizes!

I recommend no meat for children until the age of ten or eleven. Not only is it bad for a child under that age to eat meat, but also the meat that we get today in the United States is loaded with all kinds of chemicals and additives. After the child has gone through puberty, start him on a little bit of fish gradually. That is a very easy protein to digest. Do that maybe once a week. Then gradually start eating meat maybe once a week, but no more.

Today, one of the biggest contributors to our problems with heart disease and cancer is our high-fat diet. Even the Bible talks about high consumption of fat, and most of it comes from our beef and pork. (See Leviticus 3:1)

Today so many men—very young men—are having heart problems. They like their meat and potatoes. But at what cost? We've had guys in their early twenties come into our offices who've already had triple-bypass heart operations! That used to be unheard of. I focus on men here, because women have a certain amount of estrogen in their systems until they go through menopause, so we don't hear of many women having heart problems until they reach their late forties or mid-fifties. But the men suffer heart-damaging problems with those high-fat foods and resultant cholesterol levels. Most of us, men and women both, need to cut back on the high-fat foods, and beef is first on the list to go.

Not only is the fat content of the meat causing us problems. There's also another risk factor involved as well:

> You could be getting your steak with a hidden side order of drugs. Aside from meat's potential for supplying us with more protein than we need and more saturated fat than we should have, it is insidiously giving us drugs we don't want. The majority of American livestock is routinely given sub-therapeutic doses of antibiotics such as penicillin and tetracycline. Because sub-therapeutic doses are smaller than those needed to control an actual infection, they kill off susceptible bacteria and allow resistant ones to thrive, promoting the spread of antibiotic-resistant bacteria—which is being transmitted to humans.[5]

So my advice is to find a good source of home-raised beef. Kids at a young age have a very hard time digesting beef and animal proteins. Most pediatricians don't tell you this, do they? (They leave that for those of us in the field of prevention and nutritional healthcare.) But a child's digestive system is growing and developing from birth up to probably age twelve, and their organs are not properly ready.

Beef is one of the hardest foods to digest, but a child is going to like it if his family is eating it virtually every night. If you want to be easy on your young child's digestive system, don't give him a lot of animal protein right now; wait until he gets a little bit older.

It's much better, though, to give your children meat replacements. For example, you can get pre-made veggie burgers or "garden burgers" in the frozen section of your grocery store.

### Organic Eggs
This is one of the best sources of protein for children. Other good sources are;

### Bulgur
This is just like cracked wheat. I like to use Bulgur for replacing hamburger meat in soups and chili. (I do have a chili recipe using bulgur in my Maximum Energy Cookbook; try it.) When bulgur is put into chili, it looks just like hamburger meat. It is so important, make it look good.

### Beans, Lentils and Rice
Beans are a wonderfully versatile food. They're high in protein, which makes them an excellent replacement for the animal protein that many people think they "must have." Beans, lentils and rice are inexpensive to buy and prepare, and when you use them often, you'll see a big drop in your weekly grocery bill.

## *Cooking Beans and Lentils*

The easiest way to cook beans is to soak them overnight and then simmer them when preparing the meal. Remember:

- Make sure you always wash your beans and lentils, and pick out any tiny stones or grit. Drain beans and soak in distilled water. Lentils and split peas do not need to be soaked, since they cook much more quickly than beans.
- After beans have been washed and drained, cover them with boiling water and allow them to soak for at least two hours.
- To soak overnight, make sure the beans are covered with a couple of inches of water, since they will swell significantly.[6]

## *No Pain, Better Grain*

It won't hurt you at all to replace your typical refined, heavily milled grains with the good stuff. The general principle here is to use raw, whole grains whenever possible. My recommendation is that you try kasha and see how you like it. Have you heard of it? It's a combination of seven whole grains with sesame. It has whole oats, long-grain brown rice, rye, winter wheat, triticale, raw buckwheat, barley and sesame seeds. There are recipes on the package, along with suggestions for various meal uses. Try a small bag. If your family enjoys it, then you can buy it in bulk.

### *Replacing white rice*
Use brown rice instead. But don't just think, "OK, I'm going to put brown rice in boiling water, turn it off and there's our rice." There are so many ways to cook rice. I've got a recipe for brown rice pudding—and it's excellent!

## Brown Rice Pudding

2 cups goat's milk
4 eggs, beaten
½ cup fructose
¼ tsp. blackstrap molasses
2 tsp. vanilla
2 tsp. cinnamon
4 cups cooked brown rice

Preheat oven to 350 degrees. In blender, cream together 1 cup of milk and 1 cup of rice. Mix together remaining ingredients. Stir in mixture from blender. Pour into buttered baking dish. Bake for one hour. Tastes great, hot or cold!

You can even serve that rice pudding for breakfast, it's so high in nutritional value. When you're cooking rice, you can get little bags of wild rice. It's dark brown and sometimes has veggie particles in it it's really neat. It's expensive, but I've found that taking the rice, with a little wild rice mixed into it, gives you a wonderful nutty flavor. Also, you can take any whole grain— rye, barley, buckwheat—put a handful of that in with your rice, and it cooks up great too. You're getting more nutritional value out of it, and the key to health is variety in your diet.

## *Avoid These Other Less-Than-the-Best Items*

Now it's time for me to take you on a whirlwind trip through some replacement lists. I hope my suggestions here will be helpful. Feel free to come back to them as often as necessary, to remind yourself of the healthy alternatives to the old ways of eating.

### Replacing cold sweets

I used to have a big problem with ice cream, remember? I had to find a replacement. Here's an idea: Take Thompson's seedless grapes, wash them and put them in the freezer; they're excellent as a cold-sweet replacement. We take frozen fruit and water and put it in the blender and make a frozen shake. You don't have to go to ice cream every day.

## Foster a Banana Habit

A great way to sweeten your shake—or whatever—is to use overripe bananas, peeled and frozen. In recipes I often use them instead of honey. They really do the job.

### Replacing white potatoes

When you eat white potatoes, they act as a high-glycemic carbohydrate, meaning they cause sugar levels to rise just as eating sugar does. We rarely eat white potatoes at our house. Instead, I suggest sweet potatoes because there are so many things you can do with them. They also have a very high mineral content. Another replacement for white potatoes in potato salad, which we all love, is to use one potato and two heads of cauliflower. When you boil the cauliflower and then make the potato salad, you cant tell the difference. And the cauliflower is higher in nutrients.

### Replacing lard

Instead of using lard to cook with, use organic butter, olive oil, grape seed oil, macadamia nut oil or coconut oil. The best oils are cold-pressed oils, meaning chemicals aren't used to process them.

### Replacing cow's milk

By now you know it's best to steer clear of cow's milk and use raw goat's milk. But if you must use cow's milk, you could go with non-instant, non-homogenized dry milk. Organic state certified raw milk would even be better, as long as you're sure it has no Bovine Growth Hormone in it. One such brand available at many grocers is Farmland Dairies Special Request Skim Plus. Its label proclaims, "We avoid RBST (Recombinant Bovine Somatotropin)."

### Replacing iceberg lettuce
I had grown up with iceberg lettuce in salads. But if you go to the vegetable stands, you'll find romaine lettuce, spinach, endive—all kinds of leaf lettuce you can incorporate into your salads. Use them for better nutritional value.

### Replacing black pepper
It's very hard on the colon wall. Cayenne pepper has been proven to aid ulcer healing, oddly enough. It is a lot hotter than regular pepper.

### Replacing chocolate
It can be replaced with carob. But make sure it has no caffeine— that it's straight carob.

### Replacing tuna
Use red salmon—it's now just as available as tuna at the store. Yes, you can buy it canned, which isn't as good as the frozen, but it's good.

## Nut Butter Balls

Here's a great snack recipe for kids over six. Keep them in your fridge for ready use:

> 1cup nut butter (peanut, almond or cashew)
> ¼ cup maple syrup
> ½ cup brown rice syrup
> 1 tsp. vanilla
> 1 tsp. cinnamon

1½ cups crispy rice cereal
1 cup oat bran
1 cup chopped nuts
½ cup coconut (optional)

Mix together nut butter, syrup, vanilla and cinnamon in large bowl. Stir in cereal and oat bran (I find it easier to hand mix it since it's so thick). When completely mixed, form into one-inch diameter balls and place on waxed paper. Take each ball and roll in nuts and/or coconut. Chill in refrigerator. Place five or six in individual plastic bags to store in freezer. Thaw in refrigerator for later use.

### *Replace Your Old Self!*

We've been talking quite a bit about replacements in this chapter, and I want to leave you with an encouraging word about the whole process. Remember that to *replace* means to take one thing away in order to add something else in the void that remains. Do you realize that this is an eternal principle of the spiritual life? One of the great Christian saints, the apostle Paul, said it like this:

> You were taught, with regard to your former way of life, to put off your old self, which is being corrupted by its deceitful desires; to be made new in the attitude of your minds, and to put on the new self, created to be like God in true righteousness and holiness.

Ephesians 4:22-24, NIV

The change of eating habits in you and your family can follow a similar pattern of "putting off" and "putting on." It's the focus of part III of this manual, beginning with the next section. I do believe the Almighty wants to help you accomplish this. You can all go from bad eaters to healthy eaters by His strength. Are you ready to begin the exciting process of change?

## Sample Menu for Preschoolers

Breakfast: Scrambled organic eggs; grits with natural cheese (Southern) or Cream of Wheat (Northern)
Snack: Melon
Lunch: Bean spread and cheese sandwich (cut into quarters); two fruit-sweetened cookies
Snack: High-quality yogurt
Dinner: Veggie burger with oven-baked fries; favorite steamed vegetable

## Sample Menu for School Age

Breakfast: Whole-wheat French toast with real syrup
Snack: Peanut butter balls
Lunch: Cheese-filled pasta; side vegetable
Snack: Frozen grapes or blueberries
Dinner: Meatloaf; sweet potatoes; green beans

# PART III:

## THE PROCESS: A CHANGE OF HEART AND HABITS

# 7

✳✳✳✳✳✳✳

# *Parents, Its Up to You!*

It was a cute little cartoon strip. A young mother stands at the stove with her preschooler at her feet. The child looks up and asks, "What are you cooking?" "Chicken and rice." The little girl makes a horrendous face, writhes on the floor and whines: "Bleah! Yuk! Gaak!" In the last frame the same little girl is still on the floor, calmly looking up and asking, " What's that taste like?"

### *Parental Attitudes: It's How You Think*

The mother could have reacted to her little angel's "fit" and made things so much worse. In this case, a bit of silence and unruffled patience apparently made all the difference. Mom, have you discovered the importance of your own attitude in setting the stage for good eating in your home? You are the one preparing the food and the meals. If you have a great attitude, and your husband is supporting you, then everything is going to run smoothly. You may have some ups and downs. We all do. But the key is to watch your attitude.

## *The Problem With Negative Thoughts*

Children do drink in our dispositions. Just by the mindset we convey, we set them up to approach life in certain ways. Suppose you're visiting a new neighbor and her little boy comes in and says, "Hi". His mother then makes the introduction, "This is little Johnny: he's always a mess. He's always into everything, and he's had such a hard time passing in school. - He's always making D's and F's. He never cleans up his room. He never listens. Boy, he's going to be a real problem when he becomes a teenager!"

What kind of future is little Johnny looking forward to? It will probably involve some messiness, right? He's been told by the voice of authority he is a "mess" who keeps failing.

Parents, please be careful with your negative attitudes around the kids. If you've allowed negative thoughts to hurt your chances for developing better nutrition in your family, then it's time to reverse the flow. Here are three ways to start:

*1.  Learn to control your tongue.*
Ancient wisdom tells us that the tongue can kill or nourish life. This little thing in our mouths that can curse or bless them, controls us. The Bible asks, " Does a spring of water bubble out with both fresh water and bitter water?"(James 3:11 NLT). The point is, around the home we can really ensnare ourselves by the bitter words of our mouths. We can blurt out some unbelievable things to the kids before we even realize what we've said. But, of course, once the words have flown, they can hardly be retrieved-kind of like a fired bullet.

Every once in awhile, my husband and I will go to someone's house for dinner, and the husband will say something like, "I'm glad you're here tonight, because tonight we're finally going to get a hot meal!" Such remarks cut into a marriage and create an atmosphere within the whole family- an atmosphere of putting down rather than building up. But if your family is going to take on the incredible challenge of changing its eating habits, everyone must be ready to help, support and encourage at every turn. It starts with our words.

## 2. Avoid a complaining mind-set

A complaining spirit programs us for the wrong things. Let me give an example. I remember a lady who came to our offices years ago. She was extremely overweight, but she realized she'd been filling her mind with negative thoughts, day after day, for years. She'd told herself how fat she was, how unattractive, how shabbily dressed. And if you asked her how she was, she'd pour forth with a thirty-minute recital on how bad everything was. She became the kind of person who, as my husband says, would brighten up a room- by leaving it.

But we helped her change her eating habits; she changed her attitude, and she started losing weight. "I can't tell you how much better I feel since I've eliminated those high-fat foods and the salts and the sugars!" she reported, "I'm a different person. I feel really good!"

Well, about two months later we saw her again, and she was sick. She'd gone back to her old dietary habits. We couldn't understand this until revealed how hard it was for her to "make small talk." Someone would ask her how she was doing, and she had no prepackaged, half-hour recital for a response. She had nothing to complain about. Sadly, her negative thoughts had become her best friends.

### 3. Look for the good in all situations

I heard about an interesting study done years ago. It dealt with a hundred self-made millionaires, of various ages, of various occupations, some with very little education, some with Ph.D.'s. Many came from wealthy families, others grew up in poverty. But they all had one common thread, regardless of their backgrounds. They were all "good-finders." They found the good in any situation, and they proceeded to make it better. No matter the situation, and whom they met, they had something good to say, something positive to do.

Even in a negative atmosphere, find the good. Suppose you say to your spouse, "This is terrible! I've had it with the way you always cook such unhealthy food." That's negative. The happy alternative is to say, "Honey, I love you so much. I know you're really concerned about the health of the family and I know you're doing the best you can to cook the most nutritious food possible, given our time schedule and our budget. I love you for that!" With words like that, you're going to help your mate continue to change and grow. Pretty soon you'll all be eating good, healthy food every day. It will be done peacefully with no strife.

## *How Does Stress Affect Mealtime?*

When we're under stress, our digestive system shuts down. That's why it's tough to eat and deal with a stressful situation at the same time. We get a "knot" in our stomach.

When you're under stress, it's better not to eat at all. Wait until the knot is gone, or the subject matter changes. And be sure to avoid creating knotted stomachs for your children at the dinner table!

Things NOT to deal with at mealtime-

135

- Don't talk about stressful or negative subjects; especially avoid all the rotten things that happened at work that day.

- Don't review the bad grades on your child's report card- or the tree you backed into today that caused $500 damage to the car. (Get the idea?)

- Don't watch the evening news while eating. It's usually filled with depressing and violent scenes. Our bodies do react to negative news.

Can you think of some other "no-no's" to avoid at your mealtimes?

### *The Challenge of Right Thinking*

Is the way we think about ourselves and the way we think about what we eat gong to change our choices about what we eat? Yes! The Bible tell us that "as (a man) thinketh in his heart, so is he" (Proverbs 23:7). Often we take ourselves to the woodshed, beat ourselves and tell ourselves how bad we are. People will come to see me and say, "I'm always fat. I've always had a weight problem. I never lose weight. Whenever I lose weight, I gain it right back." I look at them and respond, " Aren't you being ensnared by the words of your own mouth?" If you hold on to negative thoughts about being overweight and fat continuously, you'll get exactly what you've clung to so tightly in your mind. And you'll be depressed enough to eat everything in sight, assuring the problem continues.

No matter what the source, false beliefs need to be uncovered, recognized, shared with others, and countered with the truth. Some of the countering can be done on a purely psychological level, replacing the irrational with the more rational. On a spiritual level the process calls us to the task of replacing lies about our true nature and situation in the world with biblical

136

truths about who we are in God's love. And that is a daily process. Even though we may not feel it at first, we can begin living as if the truths are true. Feelings eventually follow reality, the reality of who God says we are... and learning to believe it comes from having it in our minds over and over until it is part of us. Our emotional reactions spring from the way we view our world, and ourselves in a significant way, our interpretations are our world.

Consider all the little quips about eating, such as: "Once over the lips, a lifetime on the hips." Those are all subliminal things that we do to our subconscious minds. My husband, who has a psychology degree from Florida State University, says we have about fifty thousand thoughts every single day hurtling through our minds. And the sobering reality is that we become a sum total of what we think about.

### *Parental Example: It's What You Do*

Our good attitudes will have to result in good actions. If you eat right- and let you children see you eating right- they are going to start doing what you do. Suppose you tell you children, " No more sodas around here: we're just going to start drinking water, some diluted fruit juice, maybe a little bit of herbal tea and then some goat's milk," yet you walk into the living room sipping a cola. You can't say, "Mommy is going to drink this, but you can't drink it." That is not going to go over.

I personally know a medical doctor who claims to be trained in matters of nutrition. She preaches about a proper diet, but continues to eat bacon and other pork products, white breads and white rice. Her husband is a junk food junkie-washing down his white biscuits and gravy with diet soda. Their twin daughters live on junk and rebellion, and have failed several times in school. I encourage you to make a commitment to healthy eating, and be real!

Training our children to eat right starts with being the best example we can be. After all, what better to model, than your own healthy diet? We have friends who are apparently doing a good job of this. One of their kids came up to me to talk the other day, and I asked about some food the youngster had eaten: "Did it have sugar in it?"

"Oh, no, ma'am, " he said, with eyes wide. "My mommy won't let us eat sugar. Sugar is bad for you. It'll rot our your teeth and make you sick. It makes you really unhealthy." They had just told me, whether they knew it or not, that their parents were doing something right. And those kids were drinking it in.

They do watch us. It is our attitude about food- it is what we eat and what we do- that they are watching. Of course, they aren't going to like everything we do and say about food. What then?

### *Avoiding Home Grown Rebellion*

"I HAVE A real picky eater at home," a mom once said to me. "Basically, I tell him that he either eats what the rest of the family eats, or he doesn't eat."

"I know it's tough," I replied. "But you don't want to become the dreaded Food Police in your family." Yes, that child will eat eventually. But he may end up looking like a concentration camp survivor in the meantime.

Certainly we need to realize that our young children like to test us. I'm not going to serve Picky Peggy a separate meal just to please her. However, we do need to learn some wise techniques, well in advance, for dealing with our finicky little ones until they get used to the kind of food that's best for them. So while you're sticking to your guns with the kids, I'll suggest a few "rebellion-avoidance principles" that can help guide your efforts:

138

### 1. Let variety and creativity reign in your meal preparation

In changing your family's way of eating, remember these words: variety and creativity. When I say variety, I'm referring to what you buy and how you prepare it. Let me give you an example. I've figured out seven ways to prepare a carrot: eat it raw, shred it, juice it, steam it, bake it, boil it or cook it until it's done and grind it into baby food. Do you have any other ideas?

It's not what we eat that gets us into so much trouble; it's what we don't eat. That's why variety is so important. Then the creativity makes getting all those nutrients a pleasurable experience.

Yet it's this idea of creativity that generates so many excuses at my cooking workshops. Frankly, I refuse to listen. It's just that I've seen too many mothers and wives who work good results with little or no rebellion. I realize that "not having enough time" seems like a problem, but making food preparation a priority can overcome that obstacle. In fact, I suggest you make food preparation one of the top priorities in your life. Think about the crucial benefits to yourself and your family. You may have to give up things you've been doing for a long time in order to take care of yourselves and extend your years together.

### 2. Limit the junk food snacking habits

Children have picked up on our habits here, too. According to one nutrition writer, three-quarters of adult Americans have bedtime snacks. Throw in our constant coffee breaking and nibbling throughout the day before bedtime, you can understand why one-fourth of the average thirteen-year-old caloric intake comes from snacking. It's a habit most of us find hard to break.

The best defense is simply to stop bringing junk food into your home. Just don't buy it. Talk to the children on their level, and explain to them the dangers of a bad diet. Explain the problems with sugar. Maybe even share with them how the incidence of juvenile diabetes has risen off the charts.

It's critical that you recognize that your child can be thin and still be eating all wrong. I'm not just referring to over weight kids when it comes to snacking. We can't assume that our skinny child can eat anything she wants. I'll give you an adult example, but it applies to every one of us. Jim Fixx was a marathon runner who died several years ago. He used to run ten miles a day and competed regularly in twenty- thirty –mile- marathons.

Fixx was a thin man. He would boast about how he could eat anything he wanted to eat and not gain weight because he exercised so much. Sadly, he died in his early fifties. When they autopsied him, doctors found all of his coronary arteries severely blocked. It was frustrating, because here was a young man, the picture of health, smiling at us on TV commercials. I say these things not to criticize Mr. Fixx. He was a respected athlete and, I'm sure, beloved by his family. My simple point is that we must begin as early as possible to teach our kids to eat right, whether we think they are overweight or not. Dr. Charlie Attwood, a respected pediatrician in Louisiana, once told my husband he has never examined a nineteen-year-old teenager who did not already have the beginnings of clogged arteries and heart disease. Friends, what are we doing to our children?

It's easiest to teach good eating habits if you begin when your child is young. It gets progressively harder as kids get older. " If at age two kids are given a lot of fruits, vegetables and grains, and if they are not inundated with fried foods and cookies, they're a lot more likely to continue eating those healthy foods," (says Mary Abbott Hess, a former president of the American Dietetic Association). "But if they see adults in their environment skipping breakfast, eating a doughnut at midmorning, eating nothing but cheeseburgers and French fries

140

at lunch, and constantly talking about dieting, they're going to get those messages, too."

### 3. Learn what works with your picky eater.
Most of us have had a finicky eater at home, or we at least know a relative or neighbor who has one. In fact, at some stage of their development, most of our children will rebel at the dinner table. Do you recognize this scene?

Mother begs and pushes her daughter to eat something. When all else fails, Mom dashes to the kitchen to cook a backup, Dad, already agitated, takes his frustration out on the other kids, yelling at one for not sitting still and at the other for looking like a hoodlum. Mom gets mad at her husband for losing his cool. Who would want to be at that table? [4]

We need to know how to respond, well in advance, to that well-worn scenario. Here are some suggestions I've gathered from my own experience, from other parents and from the so-called "experts":

- *Determine to stay calm and cheerful.* A good sense of humor can go a long way when your child is having a tantrum at the table. Why not stop and enjoy the behavior for a moment? After all, when viewed objectively it can be truly entertaining.

- *Just modify what your child already likes.* Let's say you're going to make a salad for your family. Find out what vegetables the kids do like, and put those in it. Don't make dinner a complaining-and- rebellion event. It doesn't have to be that way.

- *Never use food as a reward or punishment.* Your picky eater is already responding emotionally to food and you will strengthen this tendency by attaching your love (or its

141

withdrawal) to what's on the plate. And avoid using food as a pacifier as well; it can only lead to overeating.

- *Offer to let your child help with cooking*. Knowing she had a part in making the so-called "icky" food will definitely entice your little one into trying a few bites, especially as other family members praise her excellent efforts in the kitchen.

- *Keep portions small for the "yucky" stuff*. Just offer a little sample. It's hard for any of us to be told to eat a heaping helping of a least-favorite meal. And, of course, some foods require a little time to win us over.

- *Offer multiple choices just in case everyone doesn't like everything that's been prepared*. Example: When our son Austin was young, he didn't like onions. Well, a lot of folks don't like onions, so I always make this an option. But be careful; let them choose two of the three vegetables offered. Many children would choose no veggies at all- and that's not healthy.

### *Avoid Force Feeding*

Your child's ability to like some foods but not others may depend on her genetic makeup. Also, sometimes illness or allergies interfere with the ability to taste or smell certain foods. But mostly, children learn to eat foods that they are repeatedly exposed to. If you and your spouse enjoy mealtime, so will your children. But if you force them to eat, they'll develop negative associations with food and lose their ability to judge whether they are hungry.

- When possible, offer a nutritional equivalent. Often you can exchange a particular food your child doesn't care for. Your main concern is to provide equivalent nutrients while limiting the sugar, fat and white flour.

- Consider "reverse psychology" if little Sally says, "I don't like this, " just respond, "Ok, you don't have to eat it if you don't want to; I'll put it in the refrigerator for later." But offer no replacement. When Sally is hungry before bedtime, the dish in question may start looking pretty appetizing.

### *Trying a Unique Approach*

I WANT TO encourage you to keep being creative as you go. I know it's frustrating when you want to make dietary changes and five other family members begin questioning your sanity. My husband, Ted, chose to prevent this in a rather unique way. He began praying for a certain kind of wife. Several of the attributes he asked God for was somebody who was interested in diet and nutrition. Several weeks later he was dating the answer from the Lord- me!

God provided me with the perfect companion for my lifetime, too. You see, He always answers our prayers in accordance with His will. And we know that helping our families eat right is exactly what God wants us to do. We can let Him lead us, avoiding strife in the household, as He makes the necessary changes. It will all come about according to His absolutely perfect timing, in His gentle way.

# 8

✴✴✴✴✴✴✴

# *Surviving the Supermarket Safari*

I LOVE TO shop. I don't know many women who don't like to shop. For clothes, I mean, and plenty of other things.

When it comes to grocery shopping, though, it's a different story. Trudging up and down overly air-conditioned aisles. Standing in line gazing at headlines exclaiming things like, " Boy from Mars Eats Man's Truck!" or " Face of Elvis Appears on Cheeseburger!"

None of this exactly thrills my soul.

## *Lets Go Shopping!*

Then there's the matter of having to look at all that packaged "junk" inviting me-sorely-tempting me- to get fat.

It's true: Some days I dread going to the store.

But I'm going shopping with you today. Yes, grocery shopping. We're going to take that dreaded walk down shiny tile floors and look closely at the colorfully packaged items passing by to the right and left. We'll have a great time, and I'm hoping that this little exercise will help make your future forays into grocery land so much easier and quicker. Actually, the kids will love helping you identify the "no-no's" I will be taking you down each aisle of my local store. Your grocery store will probably be set up differently, but the overall grouping of foods, are the same. First, two general principles to keep in mind as you go:

### <u>Go Organic, With Creative Spending</u>

A Harris poll of 1,250 adults throughout the United States shows that a large majority of American consumers would choose organically grown food over chemically grown food if the price were the same. Eighty-four percent of those surveyed said they would choose organically grown food if they had the option; 12 percent said they would not. Four percent were unsure. Forty-nine percent said they would pay more for organically grown food.

Years ago, I wasn't adamant about buying organically grown food, because I didn't know as much about the issue as most consumers. I used to make that my priority too, but the more I learned about the chemicals and additives in our food, the more skilled I became at "creative spending."

145

What do I mean? Creative spending is increasing the money we spend on good food by spending less on pricey junk food. In other words, we take the extra money saved from refusing the junk, and we put it toward buying organic. This means we're investing in foods that are beneficial to our health, not just appealing to our stomach.

The nice thing is that organic food production is on the increase. Farmers want to keep their soil alive and productive, and the demand is rising for foods grown without toxic chemicals. One western Massachusetts vegetable grower discovered, after fifteen years of chemical farming, that his land was dead. He realized that if there was any hope for reviving his farmland, he would have to start initiating organic farming practices. His soil looked nothing like it did when he stared farming. Not an earthworm could be found in the rock-hard soil. Today, the formerly chemical-dependent farmer is a successful organic food producer with fertile and productive soil.

Certified, organically grown produce has to be grown in soil that has had no pesticides on the land for at least three years. Then the soil is worked back to a natural state. If you are going to start buying organic fruits and vegetables, start replacing the items that usually have the highest amounts of pesticides residues: apples, strawberries, broccoli, peaches, grapes, pears, spinach.

In section two, we talked about the risks to your child's health due to pesticides, so by now I hope I have given you some enthusiasm for the organic alternative. For your family's sake, find places in your food budget where you can cut costs and use the savings toward organically grown food whenever possible.

## Where to shop?

### My first choice: Whole-food markets
Many health-food stores have come a long way since the 1960s and 1970s. In larger populated areas we are now seeing whole food markets and natural food stores replacing the old health-food stores.

Whole-food markets offer organic vegetables, bakeries and delis and a large selection of natural foods and personal care items.

Living in Florida, I can recommend the following stores where I personally shop: You may have to scout around a bit in your area, but because of the health benefits, it will be worth your trouble!

*Orlando*: Chamberlain's Hwy. 17-92, Exit 45 off of I-4

*Tampa:* Nature's Harvest, Mc Dill Ave., and Exit Howard-Armenia off of Hwy. 275

*Tampa-* Wild Oaks Market 813-874-9435, 1548 N. Dale Mabry Hwy, Tampa, FL  33607

### My second choice: Local organic produces markets
Organic produce markets offer a great selection of organic and locally grown produce. Some also offer a line of natural foods.

In the Winter Haven – Lakeland area where I live, I'm blessed to have an excellent organic market:
Pinecrest Farms, Hwy. 17 Winter Haven.

***My third choice: Local cleanest grocery store.***
The reason I say the "cleanest" is because the cleanest usually means the most frequently shopped and, hopefully, the freshest produce.

A final note: don't forget the mail-order option. I order several items from a wonderful organic mail order farm: Arrowhead Mills, 1-800-434-4246.

## *Always Go With a Firm Agenda*

THE SECOND GENERAL principle to keep in mind before you and I head to the grocery store together is this: Make sure you bring a shopping list- and stick to it. We will go shopping down each individual aisle in just a moment. I'll be sharing with you my "first choices," and I will be naming some specific brands that I use, which may be available in your area. (You see, our office receives so many calls asking, "What brand do the Broer's use?") You may find brands you like better or that save you more money. Great! But for now, grab a cart, and let's go…

### *The Dairy Aisle*

Item: Milk
First choice –raw, goat certificate organic milk
Second choice –nonfat, dry organic goat, dry organic
Third choice- low-fat organic cow milk
I admit that raw, certificate goat milk is hard to find. The nonfat, dry organic brand I use is more readily available (and convenient since you can make up a quart at a time whenever needed.) The raw milk and nonfat milk dry milk are also non-homogenized. Milk should be used in moderation in recipes or over oatmeal or cereal.

Milk purchased in your local grocery store is usually from cows and loaded with hormones, antibiotics and steroids. Now, we as health-conscious consumers have to be concerned about the new Bovine Growth Hormone. (BGH) being administered to dairy cows. The January 1996 issue of the *International Journal of Health Services* released a study concluding that consuming milk from cows treated with BGH increased the risk of breast and colon cancer.

Item: Buttermilk
First choice- organic (powdered buttermilk)
Second choice- grocery store variety

Item: Butter
First choice- raw, organic
Second choice- organic
Third choice- grocery store variety; lighted salted

I use buttermilk in a few recipes, but we don't purchase it just to drink as a beverage. Always buy butter with the lightest color, which usually means no artificial colors have been added. I always buy lightly salted for better flavor. Butter is better than margarine because margarine is a trans fat (Trans fatty acid) or hydrogenated oil. These trans fats, according to the Harvard School of Public Health, contribute to thirty thousand deaths from coronary artery disease in the United States each year.

Item: Cheese
Favorite brand- Organic Valley
First choice- raw, organic
Second choice- organic
Third choice- cheese with only milk cultures and salt

Avoid processed cheeses that contain emulsifiers, lactic acid, colorings and preservatives. Avoid cheese slices. Purchase cheese in small block rectangles, very light in color.

Item: Cottage Cheese
Favorite brand- Organic Valley
First choice- organic, low- fat
Second choice- I'll do without

Make sure your cottage cheese contains live cultures, lactobacillus, bulguricus and streptococcus thermophilus. These live cultures are especially valuable for those taking antibiotics. The cultures help replenish important intestinal bacteria that antibiotics destroy. We also offer a great product to replenish intestinal bacteria, Probiotic Blend. You can purchase this from our office or our website. 1-800-726-1834 or www.healthmasters.com

Item: Yogurt
Favorite brand- Horizon, Brown Cow, Stonyfield Farms
First choice- raw or organic sweetened with fruit juice
Second choice- any brand with no preservatives

Make sure yogurt contains live cultures, just like the cottage cheese. These cultures aid digestion and make milk more digestible for lactose- intolerant consumers.

Item: Eggs
First choice: organic, natural "yard eggs"
Second choice: grocery store natural eggs, antibiotic free

Avoid eggs containing hormones, steroids and antibiotics. With factory-produced eggs, where there is an assembly line, the factories are incredible. The chickens are producing twenty- four hours a day. God didn't intend for these little animals to do that! The lights in the hen houses are on all day and night. The drugs in those chickens may keep them from getting sick and dying. But the store eggs contain those same drugs when you eat them.

Some folks may have neighbors or friends who raise egg- laying hens that actually get to peck the ground, eat worms and bugs and see a real, live rooster. These are healthy chickens, and they lay good eggs. Their yolks are more yellow. Lecithin is actually still left in those eggs! And the shell of the egg is even harder because there's more calcium in it. Offer a fair price for such eggs, and enjoy them. High-qualify yard eggs are an excellent source of protein as long as you're eating a low-cholesterol diet otherwise.

### Canned Goods Aisle

I use very few canned goods from the grocery store- only in an emergency. That's why this section is very short. You can whiz right through this aisle. (I do use organic goods that have special, coated interiors protecting any lead seams.)

Item: Canned soups
Favorite brand- Health Valley, Organic

Item: Canned fruit
Favorite brand- Walnut Acres

Item: Crushed pineapple
First choice- buy a whole pineapple and crush it yourself

Item: Canned salmon
Favorite brand- Chicken of the Sea

### Mexican and Italian Food Aisle

Item: Canned bean dip
Favorite brand- Bearitos brand, organic

Item: Taco sauce or picante

First choice- any organic brand
Second choice- look for grocery brands with no preservatives or additives

Item: Pasta sauce
First choice- Milina, organic
Second choice- "classic," all natural

Item: Pasta
First choice-stores are offering fresh pasta now!

### *Condiment Aisle*

Item: Mayonnaise
Favorite brand- Hains Safflower Mayonnaise
First choice- I don't but mayonnaise in the grocery store.

Item: Ketchup
Favorite brand- Westbre or Hains (I like pop lids)
First choice- I don't buy ketchup in the grocery store.

Item: Mustard
First choice- any natural brand with no additives

Item: Tamari sauce
First choice- only natural brand

Item: Worcestershire sauce
Favorite brand-Robbies (or any health-food store brand)

Item: Peanut butter
First choice-fresh ground
Second choice- other good brands that contain only peanuts and salt.

Item: Jelly

First choice- any organic brand
Second choice- good grocery store brands containing only fruit, little sugar and no additives


## *Baking Good Aisle*

Item: Flour
Favorite brand- Arrowhead Mills

Item: Baking powder
First choice- a non-aluminum brand

Item: Sweeteners
Favorite brand- Scanat, date sugar
First choice- Stevia, Agave Nector, Brown Rice Syrup, fructose, raw sugar
Second choice-honey

Item: Biscuit mix
Favorite brand- Arrowhead Mills

Item: Cookie mix
Favorite brand- Arrowhead Mills

Item: Cake mix
First choice-any health food store brand with good ingredients


## *Coffee, Tea, Cereal Aisle*

Item: Coffee
Favorite brands- coffee substitutes: Roma Cappuccino, Roma, Sipp
First choice- other coffee substitutes

Item: Teas
Favorite brand- Celestial Seasonings
First choice- caffeine-free herbal tea

Item: Cereal
Favorite brand- Simply Fiber, 12 grams of fiber
Favorite brand- New Friends by Kashi, 8 grams of fiber
Favorite brand- Grainfield Raisin, 7 grams of fiber
Favorite brand- Arrowhead Mills bite-sized shredded wheat, 6 grams of fiber
First choice- brands highest in fiber, with no hydrogenated oils, or any other additives.

Item: Oatmeal
Favorite brand- Arrowhead Mills (old-fashioned, non-instant)

Item: Grits
Favorite brand-Arrowhead Mills

Item: Toaster-pastry
Favorite brand- Barbara's Nature's Choice, many flavors


*Meat Counter*

Item: Chicken
First choice- Shelton free range. Perdue claims to raise hormone-free chickens. They have an 800# you can call, 1-800-473-7383.


Item : Beef
First choice- Farm-raised local, leanest possible
Second choice- beef in moderation


Item: Seafood

See clean list on page 68. Remember, do not eat shellfish or lobster!
First choice- Salmon
Second choice-Orange Roughy
Third choice- Grouper
Fourth choice- Trout

Item: Hot dogs
First choice- salmon dogs by Aqua-cuisine, in whole food markets.
Second choice- None. I've never been able to find hot dogs in a grocery store without nitrates. Whole-food markets carry brands, but they are high in fat.

Item: Bologna replacement
Favorite brand- Yves Deli Slices (tastes just like bologna, available in most whole food markets. They also make an excellent hot dog replacement that is high in protein.

### Frozen Food Aisle

Item: Fruits and vegetables
Favorite brand- Cascadian Organic

Item: Meatballs
Favorite brand-Shelton

Item: Taquitos (corn enchilada)
Favorite brand- Senior Felix

Item: Pot pie and apple pie
Favorite brand- Amy's

Item: Pizza
Favorite brand- Amy's
### Bread, Crackers, Cookies and Chips Aisle

Item: Bread
Favorite brand- Tree of Life Seven Grain, Ezekiel bread, Seven-sprouted Grain Bread
First choice- any whole-grain bread containing no hydrogenated oils, monoglycerides, diglycerides or other preservations

Item: Crackers
Favorite brand-Ritz look-alike by Tree of Life, Saltines by Barbara's
First choice- Any whole-grain cracker containing no hydrogenated oils, monoglycerides, diglycerides or other preservatives.

Item: Cookie
Favorite brand- fat-free vanilla wafers by Barbara's
First choice- any cookie not containing hydrogenated oil, monoglycerides, diglycerides or other preservations.

Item: Chips
Favorite brand- Bearito corn chips

Item: Popcorn, microwave
Favorite brand- Bearito contains non-hydrogenated oil.
First choice- try several types and find your own favorite. We don't keep these in the house all the time.

Wow, that was a quick trip, wasn't it? Once you learn which brands are healthy and which brands you need to avoid, grocery shopping will become easier each time you do it. And speaking of avoidance, you do need to be careful on your grocery shopping adventures. There are definitely some things to stay away from.

## Lets Be Careful, Too!

Yes, now that we've taken a quick trip to the grocery store we can go back and consider some of the dangers that may lurk amidst those sparkling clean aisles. They have to do with overall safety in shopping, food preparing and learning to read those bothersome, tiny-print labels.

## Safety First!

Do practice safe shopping and food preparation to the best of your ability. What do I mean? At the most basic level, it's simply a matter of learning to think about bacteria. Just because you can't see the little creatures doesn't mean they'll leave you alone. At the store, as you make your choices, use sight, touch and smell to check for freshness; buy a good veggie spray to use on all your fruits and vegetable when you get them home. We offer a GSE concentrate that works great as a veggie wash.

## Purchasing Vegetables

We've always heard" fresh is the best," and this is so true in purchasing vegetables. Buy them in this order:

### First: Fresh
Always try to buy vegetables that are in season. Don't be afraid to try some you've never tried before. Most people eat their favorite few vegetables year after year. There are over 150 different vegetables from which to choose. Fresh vegetables should be purchased at a farmers market, private stand or co-op.

Always wash vegetables with a biodegradable cleanser. This is supposed to strip off some water repellant chemicals, but not wax. When washed properly, the skin and peeling can be consumed. (Note: The wax is a big problem with apples; either buy organic, or always peel them!)

157

### Second: Frozen

When certain vegetables are out of season, you'll have to resort to frozen. Vitamins are lost in the freezing process, but the minerals are still available. Home- grown vegetables are much better than the store-bought frozen because of the industrial manufacturing process. If you do buy frozen, buy the brands that have no sugar or salt added, such as Cascadian Farms.

### Third: Canned

Use canned vegetables as little as possible, massive amounts of salt and sugar are added. After the canning process is finished, the vegetable has very little nutritional value. You see, bacteria love food, and once the wrong kind gets into your body's system, they cause problems in our digestion- especially for children. So when you get your food home, wash your hands thoroughly before handling fresh, unpacked foods. In the kitchen, be sure to keep your dishes and utensils clean. Wash all countertops with bacteria killing bleach solution or commercial cleansers, being especially careful about this after handling meats, raw eggs or banana's. When thawing food, keep it in the refrigerator. You can avoid the " danger zone", by keeping cooked foods out on the table for only so long. Then keep them at the proper temperatures to prevent the growth of bacteria before they become your leftovers for another meal. Remember that mixtures of foods, like potato salads, should be refrigerated immediately after you make them. When you take them to the beach keep those items in a cooler with plenty of ice.

### Temperature Safety

An important rule is to keep food out of the "danger zone" the 40° to 140° window in which bacteria can proliferate rapidly on many foods. Therefore, never defrost meat or poultry at room temperature.

158

- The safest way to defrost is in the refrigerator or microwave. If you defrost in cold water, make sure there are no tears in the plastic wrap before fully immersing the item in cold water. Change the water every thirty minutes until the item is defrosted.

- Food should be cooked immediately after defrosting; don't place defrosted food in the refrigerator to be cooked later.

- Pre-chill salad ingredients, salmon, hard-boiled eggs and cooked pasta before preparing and serving. Any bacteria that find their way into these dishes will have a harder time multiplying if the food is cold.

- For the same reason, whole watermelons and cantaloupes should be placed in the refrigerated or on ice before being used. Melons should be consumed within four hours of being cut open.

When it comes to avoiding food-borne illnesses in your children, one critical strategy is easy to enforce with your kids: hand-washing. How can we get our children to establish the hand-washing habit? Maybe it takes scaring the parents! Here's a story I came across in a book titled *Safe Eating*. I'll just summarize.

Annie Condit was a freshman at New York's Oneonta State University in 1979. At the beginning of the semester, each student was given a " mystery microbe," which they were assigned to identify at the end of the course. Annie decided to compare her microbe to the ordinary microbes found on people's hands. She chose a particular morning to begin and went through the entire day without washing her hands until late in the afternoon. She recalled touching and handling all the kinds of objects she normally encountered on an ordinary day. Then she went to the lab to see what she'd picked up. First, she set up four petri dishes that contained what's known as a "growth medium," a gel-like substance. In dish 1, Annie pushed her unwashed fingers. Then she went to the sink and rinsed her hands under cold, water drying them on a paper towel. She returned and pressed her fingers onto the gel of dish. 2. After that, she washed her hands with soap and water for about a half minute, dried them with a paper towel and returned to touch dish 3. Finally, before touching dish 4, she did a "full surgeon's scrub" with antiseptic soap. She used a brush to clean between her fingers and under her nails; she even scrubbed her wrists and forearms up to the elbow.

Now Annie placed the petri dishes in an incubator and waited forty-eight hours before examining them. She was truly surprised.

Upon inspecting the results with her naked eye and under a microscope, Annie was astonished. There were hundreds of thousands of colonies of bacteria in dishes 1 and 2, leading Annie to conclude that simply rinsing with water did nothing to remove the day's worth of microorganisms that had been teaming on her skin. By comparison, there was almost nothing growing in dish 3, and dish 4 was clean. " There was maybe a five colony difference between dishes 3 and 4, Annie recalls. She photographed her results, wrote up her findings, and displayed them on a poster in the lab for other students to see. Since then, she says, "I've been a hand-washing freak."

A study published in the May 1997 issue of *Family Medicine,* concluded that school-age children, who followed a schedule of washing their hands at least four times a day, experienced fewer sick days due to gastrointestinal (GI) symptoms (nausea, vomiting diarrhea, abdominal cramps) compared with a control group that followed no particular hand-washing schedule. While it is impossible to know whether those GI symptoms had been food-borne, gastrointestinal distress is a hallmark of most food-borne infections.

One other note: When implementing better hand-washing practices in your family, consider using the pump-handle liquid soap instead of bar soap. Studies have shown that bacteria can even grow on bar soap. (By the way, did you know that soap and water don't actually kill the bacteria? They simply create a slippery surface so the little critters can slide right off?)

## *Preparing Vegetables*

I have found that certain vegetables taste better, depending on how they are prepared. There may be a vegetable your family doesn't like, but if prepared differently, they may enjoy that vegetable. Below I've taken certain vegetables and prepared them in different ways, hoping you can find that special way for each member in your family.

### *Raw Vegetables*
Raw vegetables, aid in rapidly detoxifying the body. Because of their high-fiber content, they keep the intestinal tract swept clean. That's why they're sometimes called "intestinal brooms." If your digestive system is in good working condition, raw vegetables can be very beneficial. Some children and some senior citizens may not benefit as greatly because of their inability to chew and digest properly.

### *Juicing Vegetables*
The consumption of fresh vegetable juice is the best way to receive important needed enzymes, vitamins and minerals. Juices are easily digested and add variety to your diet.

Some excellent vegetables to juice are carrots, cabbage, celery and parsley. Carrots are very high in beta-carotene, which is a precursor of Vitamin A.

Juices are the most beneficial when prepared on a daily basis, since they lose their nutritional value when exposed to air, they should be sealed tightly and kept in the refrigerator. Be creative; mix several juices together for variety.

### Steaming Vegetables
Steaming vegetables is another way to go. Foldable stainless steel steamers can be purchased in your local grocery store. To steam vegetables, place one-half to one inch of water in pot. Place your vegetables in a steamer, bring the water to a boil. Cover the pot, reduce heat and steam until tender (not mushy).

### Simmering Vegetables
It's best to start with very little water when cooking vegetables and add more water later if needed: Add one inch of water to pot (to increase mineral uptake add one-half teaspoon blackstrap molasses). Add vegetables and cover. Simmer until tender (not mushy).

### Stir-frying Vegetables
This is my favorite way of preparing vegetables. Don't feel you need to purchase a wok in order to do it, though. I do all my stir-fry in a cast-iron skillet. If you do use a wok, the best type is a stainless steel.

Advantages of stir-frying: 1.) It's the best way to prepare a balanced vegetable dish. 2.) Vegetables retain most of their crispness and are never overcooked.

### Baking Vegetables
Most vegetables that are baked are in some sort of casserole, except certain types of squash and sweet potatoes. When baking

squash or pumpkin, save the seeds. The seeds can be washed and baked on a cookie sheet and basted with a little butter. This makes an excellent snack.

## *Learn to Read Those Labels*

Have you found yourself reading labels a lot more closely since you've been shopping with wisdom? I certainly do more than glance at them these days, and I suggest you do the same. The first thing to know is that ingredients are listed in the order of concentration. For instance, if sugar is first on the list that means there is more sugar than anything else in the produce. That's right. A lot of cereal manufactures have disguised the word " sugar" with " corn syrup" "high-fructose syrup" and other names, so sugar may become the second ingredient. But the other sugars, along with the actual sugar, make it the main ingredient. The labeling laws are very lenient today in America, and that's what makes label reading such a challenge for us today.

## *A Labeling Glossary*

How well do you know your *labelese*? Check out these definitions:

*Enriched-* Describes the process of adding back in at least some of the nutrients lost during processing. Chemical vitamins are used.

*Fortified-* These foods contain added chemical vitamins and minerals that were not originally in the food (or were present in smaller amounts).

*Imitation-* A food that has had its formula altered so that it has less nutritional value than the product it resembles.

*Light or "lite"*- A virtually meaningless term. Can refer to reduced calories, but may also refer to pale color, low-sodium, taste or fluffy texture.

*Low-calorie*- The food must contain less than 40 calories per serving and less than 0.4 calories per gram.

*Natural*- When applied to meat or poultry, it means the food is minimally processed and free of artificial ingredients. But for other foods, "natural" has no legal meaning.

*Organic*- A term that has no legal meaning. The USDA, however, does not allow it to be used on meat or poultry.

*Reduced calorie*- These foods must have at least one-third fewer calories than the regular preparation. The nutritional comparison must be shown on the label.

*Sugarless and sugar-free*- Products must not contain sucrose, but they still can contain honey, glucose, and fructose or sugar alcohols such as Xylitol or Sorbitol. (Caution: More and more "sugar-free" may mean NutraSweet or Splenda replaces the sugar.)

The easy way out would be to believe that the manufacturers are actually concerned about you and your family's health and that they would never remove or add anything to your food that would harm you. Unfortunately, this is not true. As concerned consumers we must make it our responsibility to become educated on this subject.

A food label is a contract between the consumer and the manufacturer, but like many contracts, it may be difficult to understand. And what is not included may be as important as what is included. So beware of the attempt to mislead. A bag of cookies that blazes with the words no cholesterol, in bright, yellow lettering may seem like a wonderful find.

However, those supposedly healthy little morsels may be terribly high in saturated fats, sugar and salt. You'll only find that fact in the ingredient list (in decidedly smaller lettering.)

Please, watch out for such marketing ploys. My advice is straightforward here: Just refuse to put stock in health claims on labels. It's that simple. A food may have certain nutritional benefits and may supply certain vitamins and minerals, but no food is going to " make you healthy" all by itself. Some of the claims for a particular nutrient will mislead you by hyping that one thing, while leaving unsaid the fact that the product is filled with fat, sugar or additives. And even when the nutrient is indeed present in the advertised amount, what proof is there of its remaining ability to be absorbed into your system after excessive processing? Beware!

It's true that new nutrition laws from the FDA are spelling out what terms food producers can use on their products and limiting the claims that have long been made. For that we can be thankful. For example, the FDA specifically describes the definitions allowed for *fresh, healthy, lean, reduced, light, more, free* and so forth. Yet the claims are still of little value when we're attempting to raise our children to eat right. Your job and mine is simply to go beyond the advertising on the packages and look closely at the ingredients and their concentrations.

# 9

✳✳✳✳✳✳✳

# *Step by Step to a Healthier, Happier Family*

I DON'T KNOW who said it first, but it rings a bell with me: "I can't resist everything... except temptation." Ever feel that way when it comes to your food choices?

The trouble is, we like the way we're eating. We choose things that taste good to us mainly out of habit. And having grown accustomed to certain tastes, we find convenient ways to keep experiencing them. What I'm asking you to do in this book is to help your children change their habitual ways of approaching food. It involves dealing with some entrenched habits and replacing them with a whole new approach to life.

## *Confronting the Old Habits*

When it comes to how we humans decide what tastes good, we're all pretty much the same. Researchers have found that all people basically crave three things, salt, sweets and fat. And they tend to avoid the sour and bitter. Recognize anyone you know? In other words, it's natural to form the high salt-sugar-fat habit. But not everything that "comes naturally" is good for us, and our kids. I'm not asking you to eliminate these things; they're all essential for a healthy body. It's just that we often eat too much of them. And we may be unaware of the healthy substitutes that can replace the unhealthy foods while delivering the same level of taste satisfaction- if we'll just get used to the new ways.

## *Craving or Hungering?*

A big barrier to habit change in our families is our food cravings. Some of us just can't seem to resist! Others hold out for a while and then give in to a rebound of binging. Still others remain coolly consistent; we regularly overeat without much of a fight. Unfortunately, the children are watching.

But did you know that our cravings are only slightly related to actual hunger? Knowing this is critical to making changes in your family. I recall reading about an experiment done by Dr. Albert Stunkard of the University of Pennsylvania. Here's the gist of it: He gathered a number of volunteers from all weight categories-some below-average weight, some average weight, some overweight. In the experiment the volunteers were fitted with a gastric measuring device consisting of a balloon inserted in the stomach and then filled with water. The device could measure stomach contractions. The subjects didn't eat for more than fifteen hours, while being asked to report when they felt hungry.

Here's the interesting thing: The below-average weight, along with the average-weight folks, reported hunger whenever their stomachs contracted. This is natural and normal. But with the overweight volunteers, there was no correlation between hunger feelings and stomach contractions.

Before we start eating healthy, it's quite hard for many of us adults, and our children, to determine when we're hungry and when we're just responding to a psychological stimulator. That tempting stimulation might be the sight of a candy bar on a TV commercial. It might be the memory of an ice cream cone we had last week. Our children may have become overly sensitive to such experiences, and they run to the refrigerator as the habitual response. It's understandable, because we know that children who've been sensitized in these ways (by the sight or thought of appetizing food) start a secretion of insulin in the pancreas. Then comes a decrease in blood sugar levels, which typically feels like "hunger," especially for sweets. And it's not " all in their heads":

The psychological temptation triggers a bodily reaction that brings about a real physiological hunger for food. This reaction is more prevalent in overweight people, especially those who have been overweight since childhood. This is another reason that you must change your child's reactions to food now, while he or she is young, to prevent this battle having to be fought for the rest of his or her life.

In light of the fact that we've been so sensitized to our cravings, most of us find it pretty hard to change. On the other hand, let's say you've taken the information in this book to heart, and you've determined to do something about your diet and the way you're going to raise your children to eat. What's next?

## *Can Will Power Help?*

Putting it into action is next, and it won't be easy. I've found that it can be done as a process, step by step. Will power does have a role to play, of course. We can build up our resistance to temptation, but we can't do it all at once, if we try that, we're going to go through heavy withdrawals, heavy detoxification, and heavy headaches. That was my experience before I learned to gradually taper off of my sugar habit. My husband, Ted, who used to drink eighteen cups of coffee a day, now prefers malted grain "coffee". But it didn't happen overnight, it takes a gradual buildup of resistance to the old habits as we switch to the new ways.

How do we teach this to our children? With great patience and sustained prayer, while keeping in mind that it is possible.

Believe it or not, anyone, even a young child can learn to develop more will power. Will power is not an innate characteristic that you are either born with or without. It is something that is learned, although most people don't know how to go about learning it….

Will power simply represents the ability to resist tempting food. I'm not just talking about psychological resistance, or "toughing it out", what we are trying to do is retrain your youngster in such a way that we break the biochemical conditioning that occurs when she is exposed to tempting food. In this regard, I have two goals in mind. We must: 1) Desensitize the child to sight and thought of tempting foods so that his body looses its typical hunger reaction to these high-calorie foods. 2) Teach the child to distinguish between real hunger and lack of it as well as between real hunger and emotional hunger.

The two points above are more easily said that done, but I want to assure you that it's worth the attempt. For me, when I find it especially difficult to eat a proper diet, I begin asking myself: How healthy do I want my children to be? How many days a year do I want to be in the doctor's office with my kids? How high do I want my family's medical bills to be this year?

Would similar questions help you stick to your plans? They all go hand in hand with the changes we've been talking about. And that's why I say it's worth it to eat right. It's worth it to experience the pain of giving up the old habits, in order to avoid the pain of sickness in our kids and our selves.

If you're struggling with these things, I feel for you. It has taken me several years to go off all the things food had to come to mean to me. But what does food mean to you these days?

> A number of years ago an earthquake in Mexico ripped an enormous hole in a prison wall. The prisoners ran out shouting to embrace the fresh air and sunshine of freedom. Within a few hours, however, most of them had come back, seeking out their old cells. No matter what its drawbacks, the prison represented security. You must say good-bye to food as a security blanket and the familiar pain caused by overeating...

> Walk through this list and identify what food has been to you—

> Is food a parent to you? Say good-bye to it.
> Is food a god or an idol? Say goodbye to it.
> Is food your best friend? Say good-bye to it.
> Is food a plaything? Say good-bye to it.
> Is food a mood-alterting drug to you? Say good-bye to it.

## *A Greater Power is Available*

I've said that willpower has a role to play in change, and we can help our children increase their resistance to bad eating habits. But will power alone cannot produce lasting change. The wise people who started the addiction programs, years ago realized this truth from the beginning. We need a greater power than ourselves to save us from ourselves

So please do not feel guilty if you have tried and tried, again and again, and failed to make much progress on you own. People often say to me, " I know what to do now, and I am going to do." Then they find themselves virtually powerless to produce any results. Has it happened to you? You've probably already learned by experiences that will power alone is never enough to bring about a lifelong transformation. It's the same with any attempt at self-improvement. No one can reach the heavenly heights by pulling on their own bootstraps.

> It is God who works in you to will and to act according to his good purpose.
>
> Philippians 2:13, NIV

So there is a place for our hard work and will power in resisting what hurts us. But even that choice is a gift from God. We do it while relying on a greater strength than our own. It is ultimately our complete dependence on divine omnipotence that carries us through.

Many of us will not be ready to change until we've hit rock bottom. It was certainly hard for me until I saw that I couldn't eat right (or do anything else) without help. No one can. And one other thing: Does it help you to know that I am not doing anything differently than what I have told you to do? I'm eating the same way I'm inviting you and your children to eat. It is not always easy at the start. Eventually, it's a piece of cake (excuse the expression).

## *Need Some Reinforcement?*

Behavior modification is a method of positive reinforcement for accomplishing habit changes. The rules are pretty straight forward, and if they help you great! Here are the five basic requirements for developing new eating and exercise habits in kids with this approach:

### *Requirement # 1*
New habits must follow a scheduled routine. A child should not be allowed to eat anything whenever he wants. Any new habit must be scheduled into a definite routine. This means regular meals at consistent times, which are calm and pleasant times, with no TV. (If a child wants to eat a healthy snack, such as fresh veggies or whole fruit, this should not be restricted.)

### *Requirement # 2*
New habits must be repeated over and over. Don't rush. Habit change takes time. The more nutritious foods will taste different and perhaps not as good at first. But with repetition and practice, the new foods will become as familiar as the old ones.

### *Requirement # 3*
Your child must learn to keep track of personal habit changes. Self-monitoring is a critical factor in changing our habits. Keep a written record of new eating habits, and post it in a prominent place.

### *Requirement # 4*
New habits must be rewarded. Reward good eating! Habits that are rewarded and rewarded immediately tend to be repeated. Rewards always work better than punishments when it comes to eating changes. Try a hug or a verbal affirmation.

*Requirement # 5*

Parents need to be in agreement and not eat food the children are told not to eat. In other words, the parents need to lead by example. Remember: If you have an overweight child, it's your responsibility to correct the problem.

One other thing: I've always heard that if you practice any action for thirty days it becomes a habit. So if you're hooked on ice cream, don't eat it for thirty days. Then keep it out of the house; if you don't have junk food in the house, you'll be less likely to eat it. I will admit that if it is in the house, I will want to eat it. That's why it never enters our house. It just works so much easier that way.

## *Walking Into Your New; Healthy Life!*

Now, as you work on your "habitual relationship" with food, you'll want to take some steps toward a whole new way of living healthy". It involves food, of course, but it involves so much more. Teach these principles of living to your child by word and example; you'll all grow healthier and happier together.

## *Seven Steps To a Healthy Life*

### *Step 1: Maintain a high-nutrition diet.*

Yes, it's true: You are what you eat, at least physically. And the point I've been trying to make about nutrition throughout this book is that if we want to become healthy and full of energy every day, the easiest way is not always the best way. It's just plain easy to eat all wrong.

Then we end up feeling tired, moody, depressed and anxious, wondering what's wrong with us. You probably know what it's like to deal with a child who's experiencing the same thing, the terrible lows of an improper diet! So, at the risk of becoming

173

monotonous, I repeat: it is so very important when preparing meals to use fresh vegetables, grains and fruits while cutting back on fat, sugar and processed junk. Keeping the ancient vision of "nutritional paradise" in the front of your mind may help:

> For the Lord your God is bringing you into a good land of flowing streams and pools of water, with springs that gush forth in the valleys and hills. It is a land of wheat and barley, of grapevines, fig trees, pomegranates, olives, and honey.
> Deuteronomy 8:7-8, NLT

### Step 2: Drink distilled water
Speaking of "flowing streams of water, " did you know that our bodies are composed of about 80 percent water? This should help you realize how important it is to drink plenty of good, steam-distilled water every day.

Our minds are conditioned by the media to think that "coke is it" and "Pepsi is the new generation." I look forward to the days of commercials that loudly proclaim, "Water-no sugar, no caffeine: it's the real thing!"

Most people do not drink enough water. Certainly, children rarely do. I have heard teenagers say, "Water, how boooorrrriiiinnngg!" yet I believe that if the media blared ads for water as they do for soft drink, more people would drink it, and many more would enjoy better health. It's sad to say, but the profit margins are much lower on the sales of water than on the sales of soft drinks.

### Step 3: Learn to handle the stress.
Do you know anyone who doesn't have stress these days? Today it's hard to avoid stress in our lives, so how you handle it will determine how it affects your health.

174

Believe me, it's a critical issue. Some health professionals now attribute most of our diseases to the ravaging effects of stress. We have two types of energy in our bodies: available energy and reserve energy. Available energy is what we use without any extra effort. Reserve energy is the energy stored in our body for emergencies. When the body is constantly responding to one crisis after another, it has no time to rebuild itself. Once you have "used up" most of your energy reserves, they are very difficult to replace.

How can we reduce stress? In counseling mothers, I've found some ideas that have helped reduce added stress in their lives. Consider these approaches, even if you aren't a mother:

- Identify what is causing stress. You cannot avoid the stress if you don't know what's causing it. Sometimes the real reasons lie a little deeper than the surface situation. (Consider psychological counseling if you can't seem to overcome generalized anxiety in your life over long periods of time. This may be a sign of depression.) In our Eat, Drink and Be Healthy program we have an excellent article on depression and what can be done from a natural standpoint. For more information, see the ad in the back of the manual.
- List your priorities, and then make a start in doing what's at hand to do. Don't get caught up in a cycle of procrastination and guilt.
- Learn to say "no." a woman once told me she didn't have enough time to cook nutritionally because she had such a busy schedule. I asked her to share her schedule with me. Her response: "Well, Sunday is church. Monday night is woman's club meeting (every 1st Monday.) Tuesday is bowling. Wednesday is church. Thursday night is aerobics. Friday night we go out to eat. Saturday night we usually have friends over. See? I really don't have time to cook this way."

Every now and then we must learn to say "no," or we will end up burning the candle at both ends; we will be living off our reserve energy. It is important that your family has at least four home-cooked meals a week. Not only are you and your family going to eat and feel better, but also you'll have that "quality time" to spend together, something so many families no longer have.

### Step 4: Exercise daily

One of the best ways to "unwind" after a stressful day is to exercise. Get some type of exercise three to four times a week. It can keep the blood flowing to the brain for better concentration. Exercise also helps your body stay toned while cutting the amount of body fat accumulated in the skin and around the organs. And remember: You don't have to join a sports team or gym to exercise.

When I would finish my exams in college, I would grab a friend and we'd go out to the tennis courts and just hit tennis balls back and forth for about an hour. It was great to feel the stress leave and my body loosen up at the same time. Plus I didn't have the stress of having to win or loose.

These days, my oldest son, Austin, and I take karate lessons, something we've done for the last three years. We used to go two times a week. I consider those classes, my "unwinding" time. I look forward to those afternoons, especially when I've had high-stress day. No matter how tired we are when we get home from class, we both feel better and have more energy than we did before. Plus, the mother-son relational time is great.

### Step 5: Enjoy the sunshine

We constantly hear that overexposure to the sun can be dangerous to our health. This is a true statement. But several hours of sun per week is good for your health. The ideal times to be out in the sun are before 10:00 A.M. and after 2 :00 P.M.

176

It's been proven that sunlight can lower cholesterol levels by converting the cholesterol into vitamin D. Sunlight is called "full-spectrum" light. If you work in an office all day, you probably sit under artificial lighting. But did you know that full-spectrum lighting is now available for offices? It's more expensive, but it tends to have a calming effect on those who use it.

### Step 6: Keep an upward outlook

We hear so much today about having a "positive attitude." To most of us it just sounds like "fluffy words." But think about it: the real " you" is a sum total of your thoughts. And the principle of reaping and sowing applies to the way we think. If we always sow negative thoughts, we will become a negative person. On the other hand, if we sow positive thoughts, we become a positive person.

If someone asks you, " How are you doing?" do you respond, " Not too bad"? Why not make it into a positive, and say "Quite well, thank you!" Remember, you can be snared by the words of your mouth. "This is the day which the LORD hath made; we will rejoice and be glad in it" (Ps.118: 24) Doesn't that sound better?

When preparing your family's meals, your attitude will affect how they react to the food you've prepared. You are usually the one responsible for " setting the stage."

> Kind words are like honey, sweet to the soul
> and healthy for the body.
>> Proverbs 16:24, NLT

### Step 7: Take up fasting

Fasting is one of the most effective ways of strengthening the internal organs of the body. It is also effective in helping the body to return to its genetically normal body weight. I believe very strongly in fasting because I've seen dramatic improvement in the health of those who've tried it. I talked about fasting in section four as a way of preparing for conception. But it's good for anyone who isn't pregnant. (Children should not be permitted to fast.)

I personally have gone on several seven-day cleansing programs, a very detailed program. If you're interested in this, you can contact our office. It had taken me several months to get pregnant with our son Austin. I went on a seven- day cleansing program, and I was pregnant within two months.

Fasting allows the body to take a rest, too. The digestive system can have some "time off" while the body uses energy to cleanse and strengthen the organs. When these other organs are strengthened, the body experiences are increase in the amount of food-energy available for cell repair and replacement.

Is it normal to experience headaches while fasting? When most people fast for the first few times, they do go through "toxic withdrawal." This means the body will rid itself of toxins and chemicals stored in the system. Usually the withdrawals are more severe in people who've been taking in large amounts of caffeine, sugar, alcohol, tobacco and other drugs.

Strong withdrawals may result in headaches, strong body odor, bad breath and nausea. If you are fasting for the first time, you may have some of these reactions since your body will be releasing years' worth of accumulated waste. In the "throwing off" of these wastes, withdrawal reactions are normal. Someone once told my husband, "Ted, I can't fast because I get headaches." Ted's response was, "Join the club. The same thing happened to me, but I stuck with it; it was well worth the headaches in the long run."

The point is to stick with your plans for healthier living no matter how you decide to make the changes. Taking the seven steps above should help you achieve a new level of energy, health and happiness for you and your children. If you're inspired to try them, then I say, " Go for it!"

# 10

******

# *Handling Those Special Eating Situations*

I'VE FOUND THAT when people start changing their diets, and they say to themselves, " I'm going to make sure my children eat right," they rely heavily on controlling the home environment for proper eating. Naturally!  That's how they can implement new shopping habits; make significant changes in food preparation and monitor family members' eating habits each day. Then it eventually hits them: "Oh, no! What about the approaching holiday?"

Food fear kicks in.

### *Hope for the Holidays?*

You needn't succumb to those red-letter day dietary terrors. "But the whole crowd is coming over from Aunt Martha's house!" you say. "And our relatives think we eat weird already. What am I going to cook? What am I going to do?"

I know all the "buts." And yes, they are challenging. Yet holiday horror isn't necessary, because there is a way to approach these special situations calmly and successfully. First, realize that when you're cooking for the holidays, you don't have to "eat weird." Second, remember that it's not what you eat between Christmas and New Year's that's going to hurt you. It's what you eat between New Year's and Christmas.

Think about that. What little time there is between Christmas and New Year's. And the celebrating- I'm assuming within moderation- is not going to hurt you. It's the stuff that you and your children eat day after day, week after week, all year long that's going to diminish your health over the long haul, if you're abusing your body with highly processed, highly refined sugars and junk food.

Sometimes we think that if we don't have cancer, diabetes or heart disease, we're healthy. But do you know people who have headaches, indigestion, constipation, irritability, depression and are tried all the time? So, when we talk about eating properly, you can also do it for the holidays, too. Don't be afraid to try.

### *Be a Gracious Guest*

Just recently, an elderly friend asked our family over for dinner. After discussing this with my husband, we decided we really needed to go. This dear lady was so sweet and considerate to invite us.

We had a nice visit while eating a 1 ½-inch thick hamburger on a 1-inch white bun. Afterward, we were offered vanilla ice cream. "Just a little" came back to the table as a great big bowl. If that wasn't enough to cause us to roll out of our chairs and waddle to our car, our sweet host wanted us to try a new chocolate bar she just bought. I pinched off a piece the size of my thumbnail and hoped that would be enough to satisfy her.

The next morning, I felt the price of the night before. My workout in the gym was far from productive, but what should I have expected? I had tossed and turned all night long.

Sometimes we all may have to eat things we don't really need just to be polite. But, our family never compromises when it comes to unclean meat, NutraSweet, Splenda, margarine or Olestra. There should be at least one thing you can find to eat when you are invited to dinner. Just don't make an issue over the things you don't eat.

Relax and enjoy being a guest. Are you planning to visit relatives, and won't be cooking? What I suggest, if you're really concerned about your diet, is just don't eat anything "unclean." If your host is serving pork or lobster, for instance, don't eat it. But make sure to eat a little bit of everything else.

Use your best judgment, but keep this in mind: It's worse to offend loved ones or hurt their feelings than to have a stomachache over something you're eating. That one meal you're going to be eating over the holidays is nothing compared to what you're eating all year long. Don't make a big deal out of this particular meal. Try it; eat it. And make it your goal to enjoy the fellowship.

Let's assume you'll be cooking your holiday meal for family or friend this year. You've got to make sure that the food you're preparing is good for the people you're hosting. You can do that without creating a "weird" impression or gaining a reputation for bad-tasting cuisine. Just think "alternatives and substitutes" whenever you can.

### *Food Alternatives for Thanksgiving and Christmas*

The holidays we think of for big meals are Thanksgiving and Christmas, right? And the menu centerpiece that springs to mind is turkey; everything revolves around the big bird. You may go with turkey; it's certainly better than ham (which you won't even consider). But what are the alternatives?

182

### *Replacing the traditional turkey*

Buy a kosher turkey, organically raised. If you've never tried it, you won't believe the delicious difference that surpasses the store-bought, mass-produced turkeys at your grocery. They're moister, more flavorful and just so much better.

Let me tell you why. The grocery store's mass-produced varieties are raised at a turkey farm for a profit. In other words, the turkey farmer wants to produce so many turkeys this year to make so much money. No problem with that concept. However, if you know anything about turkeys, you know they're very dumb animals. And they don't live long. But turkey farmers want as many turkeys to stay alive as possible before the holidays in order to sell them. Again, this is just Economics 101. The problem is, they're going to inject those turkeys with hormones for a "better" product, inject them with antibiotics to prevent sickness and inject them with steroids for faster growth. All of this is ingested in the animal, infused into its meat and then spread around in you.

I'm not trying to scare you; there is an alternative, and it tastes better, but without the hormones, the antibiotics and the steroids pumped in. Where do you buy organically grown turkeys? Health food stores, of course. Hebrew National carries them. You may try asking your local grocery store meat manager if he can order in organic turkeys for the Holiday season. They're more expensive, but the expense is worth it (You can also get kosher chickens; even the broth from these birds is less greasy.)

### *Replacing the corn bread dressing*

I was raised "Southern," so I'm often talking about Southern cooking. The next thing on the holiday menu down South, after the turkey, is the dressing. Usually it's corn bread dressing, very doughy because white bread is key ingredient. Now, I've already talked about white bread, but I'll just add this: Ted and I have done seminars in which we've taken white bread minus the crusts, rolled the bread up in a ball and thrown it at the wall. It bounces right back to us! Now, if it does that in the dining room, what does it do in your colon?

I use Ezekiel bread in my corn bread dressings. We've found it to be the best for keeping sugar levels pretty normal, and it's certainly healthier than white bread. The Ezekiel bread recipe comes right out of the Bible, being sprouted grain bread. It makes excellent dressing because it's not real gummy. It's got substance to it, and it is very high in protein and minerals. It's also a good bread to use in the dressing because it turns out so well. Here are a couple examples of recipes from my Maximum Energy Cookbook:

### Corny Corn Bread

| | |
|---|---|
| 1 cup fresh cornmeal | ¼ cup whole-wheat flour |
| ¼ tsp. baking soda | |
| ¼ tsp. sea salt | 1 cup low-fat milk |
| 1 small onion, chopped | |
| 2 Tbsp. butter | ½ cup pastry wheat flour |
| 2 yard eggs | |
| ¼ cup honey | ½ fresh-cut corn |

Combine first 4 ingredients together. In a blender, mix remaining ingredients except corn and onion. Stir in corn and onion. Oil and flour a glass pie plate. Bake at 350 ° for 20 minutes, or until it is slightly brown. For sweet corn bread, leave out the cut corn and onion, and add one tablespoon of sorghum. Serves 6.

### Southern Corn Bread Dressing

1 batch of corn bread
2 Tbsp. Olive oil
10 slices Ezekiel bread (or raisin bread)

1 Tbsp. Poultry seasoning
1 doz. Yard eggs, hard- boiled, chopped
1 Tbsp. Ground sage
1 large stalk celery, chopped
1 Tbsp. Parsley
2 large onions, chopped
2 tsp. Sea salt (optional)
2 to 3 cans Health Valley chicken broth
1 chopped apple
½ pecan piece

In a large skillet, sauté onions in oil. Add celery and
sauté until tender. In large bowl, crumble corn bread
and bread into fine crumbs. Add broth and mix well.
Add remaining ingredients. Mix well and spread in
large baking dish. Bake at 350° for 30 minutes, until
top starts to brown. Serves 10-12.

### *Replacing The Cranberry Sauce*
The next thing we often serve at Thanksgiving is cranberry
sauce. The cranberry sauce in the grocery store is loaded with
high-fructose corn syrup, sugar and all kinds of processed
additives. We use natural cranberry sauce, and it is excellent. It
doesn't taste like gel, and the flavor is so much stronger and
richer without all the sugar.

## *Why Do We Crave Sweets?*

Considering the sobering effects of a high sugar diet, why do we
eat so much of it? One reason is that gives us a quick infusion of
energy. It can also help to raise the level of certain brain
neurotransmitters, which may temporarily elevate our mood...
When sugary foods are consumed, the pancreas must secrete
insulin, a hormone that serves to bring blood glucose levels
down. This allows sugar to enter our cells, where it is either
burned off or stored. The constant up and downs of blood sugar

levels can become exaggerated in some individuals and cause all kinds of health problems... Our craving for sweets is not intrinsically a bad thing; however, what we reach for to satisfy that craving can dramatically determine how we feel.[1]

### Replacing The Other Holiday Side Dishes

What are some other things you have with the meal? Maybe some vegetables and sweet potatoes, right? I love sweet potatoes. White potatoes are fine every now and again, but they're part of the "nightshade family" and are low in nutritional value. They have a tendency to cause blood sugar to rise as well. On the other hand, sweet potatoes are very high in trace minerals.

I have many sweet potato recipes in my Maximum Energy Cookbook. It has a meringue recipe that's excellent for topping your sweet potatoes. You might want to try it.

### Replacing The Holiday Beverages

At my house we usually have steam-distilled water with our meals. But when I have an open house or a holiday get together, I like to have punch.

In fact, I have a Hot Christmas Punch idea for you:

- Make a little bag (I use an old, washed, and sterilized handkerchief) and put some spices in it. I put two sticks of cinnamon (broken up), 1 teaspoon of whole allspice and about ten cloves. Put them in this little bag and sew it up or tie a knot in the corners so they don't fall out.
- Put a big pot on the stove, put your bag in it, along with some apple juice and water, and bring it to a boil. The scent is wonderful! As you let it boil, the spices get into the punch. You can then pour it into a punch bowl with the punch.
- You can put a couple of sliced oranges in it while it's boiling, and then put the oranges in the bowl with the punch.

186

Another drink that we serve during the holidays is eggnog. I love eggnog, but the grocery store brands are loaded with sugars and chemicals. Alternatives? I use fresh eggs and brown rice syrup for sweetener. I put vanilla and nutmeg in it as well (or buy a natural brand, usually available at your whole-food market around the holidays).

## *When You Must Eat Out*

Occasionally your family will be eating out at a restaurant. The first rule here is to avoid fast-food places. If you knew what we know about those seemingly harmless establishments with their multi-million-dollar ad campaigns you wouldn't even think about turning into that drive-through. It's a habit for many of us, but realize that those places are not concerned about your health. That is your concern, and you are responsible for your children and they shouldn't be eating any Fun Freddy Juicy Burgers! (I know, it's convenient. But a lot of things you can prepare at home will become convenient too, once you get used to the idea.)

Of nearly 66 million Americans who eat out at least one meal a day, 33 percent choose fast-food restaurants. The New England Journal of Medicine said that nearly 40 percent to 55 percent of the typical fast-food meal is made out of fat. Even nutritious foods, such as baked potatoes, are turned to fat with added toppings such as sour cream and bacon bits. Fast-food chains spend nearly one billion a year on television advertising, and our kids eat every bite.

So crossing the fast-food joints off your list, you're left to consider the other options. Here's where my second eating out rule comes into play: Go for menu variety at " family-style" restaurants. Some restaurants specialize in one or two things: mostly steaks, grilled foods, seafood and so forth. But the restaurant for you is the one most likely to offer the healthy foods you want. It's the one where you and the kids can make substitutions most easily, sticking to low-fat dishes that can be steamed, boiled, roasted-anything but fried.

## *Tips for Eating Out*

What do you do when you and your family are eating out, and you still want to eat healthy? Do the best you can? Try these tips:
- Choose a restaurant that serves a variety of foods.
- Consider a salad bar, but avoid fat-filled, high calorie dressings.
- Ask questions about food preparation and portion sizes. ("Do you use butter or margarine?")
- If you must eat meat, try to stick to a fish like orange roughy, or salmon and make sure it is broiled, grilled, baked or steamed- not fried.
- Ask that sauces be served on the side so you can portion them out.
- Keep the meal simple; avoid fancy dishes with ingredients you are not sure of.
- Control portion sizes, and do not make your child eat everything on his plate.

(My husband and I usually split an entrée; this is one way we avoid overeating)

## *Have a Healthy Birthday!*

Birthdays usually bring to mind a long list of standard favorites; pizza, soda pop, ice cream, cake, and candy. How will your child enjoy birthday without indulging in these no-no's? You're the one to make it happen.

You can start by offering: fun food: that's healthy. Try these Funny Face Sandwich ideas (these also make great luncheons or snacks):

# Funny Face Sandwiches
## (Let the Kids Help!)

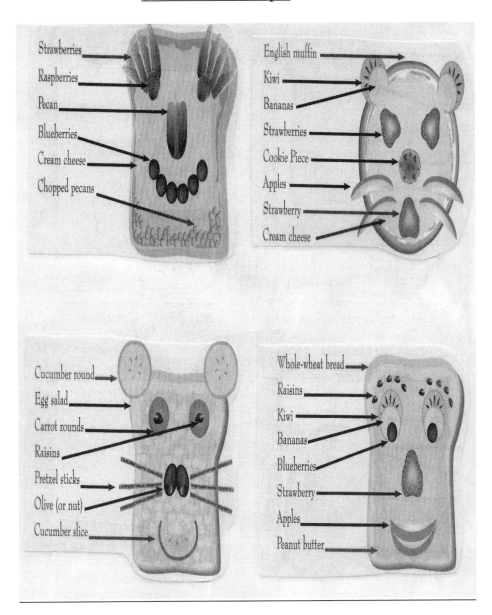

Strawberries
Raspberries
Pecan
Blueberries
Cream cheese
Chopped pecans

English muffin
Kiwi
Bananas
Strawberries
Cookie Piece
Apples
Strawberry
Cream cheese

Cucumber round
Egg salad
Carrot rounds
Raisins
Pretzel sticks
Olive (or nut)
Cucumber slice

Whole-wheat bread
Raisins
Kiwi
Bananas
Blueberries
Strawberry
Apples
Peanut butter

### *Funny Face Spreads*

Banana cream cheese
    Cream cheese
    1 banana, mashed
    ½ tsp. Vanilla
    2 Tbsp. Fructose

Cinnamon cream cheese
    Cream cheese
    ½ tsp. Ground cinnamon
    2 Tbsp. Honey

Almond-maples cream cheese
    Cream cheese
    ½ tsp. Almond extract
    2 Tbsp. Maple syrup

Mix thoroughly. These are fun, and you will probably be surprised at some of the ideas you children will think up.

When it comes to food decorating be sure you replace the standard food colorings. There are two natural colorings you can use. For instance, if you wanted to make a green-colored icing for a cake or whatever, I suggest using liquid chlorophyll, the coloring that comes from green leafy vegetables. It's in a concentrated form and is really good for you. The brand I recommend is World Organic. For red coloring, I use By Nature's Way (brand) beet capsules or powder. It's simply made of powered beets and again it doesn't change the taste.

## *Make a Start… Toward Love*

We've come to the end of this book, and I know you may still be thinking. Well, it all sounds great, but it's such a radical change from what I've been doing for so long. Your temptation may be to put this little volume on the shelf and go back to the old eating habits that are so comfortable. Change can be terribly stressful. But I urge you: Just make a start.

You can't do it all at once, and no one is expecting you to. You can't whip a U-turn with the Queen Mary! It's got to be a gradual change, because families can become rebellious, and you do need to maintain good relationships at home. But it will help to keep a heavenly perspective, to continually see yourself and your family members just as God sees you. What do I mean? Psalm 139:13-14 says:

You made all the delicate, inner parts of my body and knit me together in my mother's womb.
Thank you for making me so wonderfully complex! Your workmanship is marvelous- and how well I know it.

-NLT

Do you, indeed, know it? Are you wholly aware of, and deeply grateful for the marvelous work God has done in creating you and your children? Are you able to feel in your heart the surpassing love God holds for you, his blessed creatures?

I hope you will take some time, before doing anything else, just to bask in the warmth of His delight in you. He made you for love, and He carries you in loving arms all through your life.

# NOTES

## Chapter 1
### What's Happening to Our Children Health?

1. Phyllis Balch and James Balch, Prescription for Dietary Wellness (Garden City Park, NY: Avery Publishing Group, 19980,208.
2. Ibid, 206-207 (adapted).
3. William Dietz and Loraine Stern, eds., American Academy of Pediatrics Guide to Your Child's Nutrition (New York: Villard, 1999), 204 (adapted)
4. Charles Kuntzleman, Healthy Kids for Life ( New York: Simon Schuster, 1988), 189-190 Linda Rector- Page, Controlling Allergies and Overcoming Asthma With
5. Herbs, ( Sonora, CA: Healthy Pubs.,1996),23
6. Joseph C. Piscatella, Fat- Proof Your Child ( New York: Workman Publishing, 1997) 6-7
7. Vicki Poretta and Marcela Kogan, Mom's Guide to Your Kid's Nutrition ( New York: Alpha Books, 1997),126.
8. Kuntzleman, Healthy Kids for Life, 137
9. Poretta, Mom's Guide to Your Kid's Nutrition, 135.

## Chapter 2
### Who's Telling Them What To Eat?

1. Dietz, American Academy of Pediatrics Guide to Your Child's Nutrition, 159.
2. Robert E. Kowalski, Cholesterol and Children: A Parent's Guide to Giving Children a Future Free of Heart Disease ( New York: Harper and Row, 1988), 76-77
3. Earl Mindell, Unsafe at Any Meal (New York: Warner Books, 1987), xiv,90
4. "How Safe Is Our Produce?" Consumer Reports, March 1999, 29-30.
5. World Health Organization, "Technical Report Series," 799(1991): 40. Evaluation of certain verinary drug residues in food: $37^{th}$ report of the joint FAO/WHO Expert Committee on Food Additives.
6. National Research Council, " Toxicity testing: Strategies to determine needs and priorities" ( Washington, D.C.: National Academy Press, 1984).
7. Emilio Perez- Trallero, Mercedes Urbieta, et.al., " Antibiotics in veterinary medicine and public health " Lancet, vol. 342, Nov. 27, 1993,1371.
8. "EPA to study an insecticide for links to cancer, " New York Times, Oct. 24, 1993,21.
10. Ted Broer, Maximum Energy (Lake Mary, FL: Siloam Press, 1999), 175.
11. Carol Ann Rinzler, Nutrition for Dummies ( Foster City, CA: IDG
12. Poretta, Mom's Guide to Your Kid's Norton, 7.

## Chapter 3
### Turn Off The Tube- And Start The Day Right!

1. Poretta, Mom's Guide to Your Kid' Nutrition, 128.
2. Mindell, Unsafe at Any Meal, 20; Ruth Winters, A Consumer's Dictionary of Food Additives( New York: Three Rivers Press, 1978).
3. Food Product Development, December 1980, 36-40
4. Sheldon Margen, etal., eds., The Wellness Encyclopedia ( New York: Houghton Mifflin Company, 191), 144-145 ( adapted).

## Chapter 4
### Start With Baby... And Before

1. James Scala, Nourishing Healthy Children (Dallas: Bruce Miller Enterprises, Inc. 1988), 2-3 (adapted).
2. Lind Rodriquez, Children's Health: Problems and Solutions ( Dallas: Bruce Miller Enterprises, Inc. 1995), 4 (adapted).

3.   Scala, Nourishing Healthy Children, 4.
4.   Rodriguez, Children's Health: Problems and Solutions, 3.
5.   Scala, Nourishing Healthy Children, 4.
6.   Balch, Prescription for Dietary Wellness, 183.
7.   Ibid, 184.
8.   Ibid.


## Chapter 5
### Keep The Little Ones Eating Right

1.   Bernard Jensen, Colostrum: Life's First Food ( Escondido, CA: Self- published. 1993), 10
2.   CMA information comes from an internet article citing the following sources: (a) Gerrad JW Mackenzie, JWA, et,
3.   al., "Cow's Milk Allergy: Prevalence and Manifestations in an Unselected Series of Newborns" ACTA Paediatrica Scandinavica Supplement, vol. 234, 1973; (b) Food and Agriculture Organization of the United Nations: "Observations on the Goat: (1970); (c) McKenzie, David, Goat's Milk- It's Nutritive and Curative Value, chapter 3.
4.   Rodriquez, Children's Health: Problems and Solutions, 112 (adapted).
5.   Ibid
6.   Bernard Jensen, Goat Milk Magic: One of Life's Greatest Healing Foods (self-published, 1994), 2-3.
7.   Ibid.,3.
8.   Judith E. Brown, Nutrition and Pregnancy (Los Angeles: Lowell House, 1988), 144.


## Chapter 6
### Fuel Those Active Minds and Bodies!

1.   Mindell, Unsafe at Any Meal, 93.
2.   Ruth Elkins, Stevia: Nature's Sweetener (Pleasant Grove, UT: Woodland Publishing, 1997).
3.   Kathleen Moloney, Parents Guide to Feeding Your Kids Right ( New York: Prentice Hall, 1989), 16
4.   Balch, Prescription for Dietary Wellness, 1973.
5.   Mindell, Unsafe at Any Meal, 131.
6.   Ted Broer and Sharon Broer, Eat, Drink, and be Healthy Cookbook (Lenexa, KS. Cookbook Publishers, Inc.,1991).


## Chapter 7
### Parents, It's Up To You!

1.   Dietz American Academy of Pediatrics Guide to Your Child's Nutrition, 1.
2.   Joe Biuso and Brian Newman, Receiving Love (Colorado Springs, CO: Victor Books, 1999) ,102.
3.   Kutzleman, Healthy Kids for Life, 153.
4.   Piscatella, Fat- Proof Your Child, 159.
5.   Poretta, Mom's Guide to Your Kid's Nutrition, 72.
6.   Ibid, 74.


## Chapter 8
### Surviving the Supermarket Safari

1.   Broer, Eat, Drink and Be Healthy Cookbook
2.   David W. K. Acheson and Robin K. Levinson, Safe Eating (New York: Dell Publishing, 1988), 234.
3.   Ibid
4.   Ibid, 213.
5.   Broer, Eat, Drink, and Be Healthy Cookbook

193

6.  Margen, The Wellness Encyclopedia, 140.
7.  Ibid, 143.

## Chapter 9
### Step By Step To A Healthier, Happier Family

1.  Peter M. Miller, The Hilton Head Diet for Children and Teenagers( New York: Warner Books, 1993),54-55
2.  Ibid, 56.
3.  Ibid, 56-57.
4.  Frank Minrit, Paul Meier, et. Al., Love Hunger (New York: Ballantine Books, 1990), 106-107.
5.  Miller, The Hilton Head Diet for Children and Teenagers, 73-83 ( adapted).


## Chapter 10
### Handling Those Special Eating Situations

1.  Elkins, Stevia: Nature's Sweetener, 16,18.
2.  Poretta, Mom's Guide to Your Kid's Nutrition, 92.
2.  Miller, The Hilton Head Diet for Children and Teenagers, 139.

# *A Special Note About Our Nutritional Programs and Supplements.*

Almost every vitamin, supplement or other particular product that I've mentioned in this book can be ordered directly from our offices. You can also receive personal nutritional consultations over the phone by calling the same number. If you'd like to become more involved in a total lifestyle change toward healthy living consider these products:

TO ORDER CALL: 1-800-726-1834   WWW.HEALTHMASTERS.COM
PRICES SUBJECT TO CHANGE WITHOUT  NOTICE

~~~~~~~~~~~~~~~~~~~~~~~~~~~~~~~~~~~~~~~~~~~~~~~~~~~~~~~~

## *Eat Drink, and Be Healthy CD Program*      **$119.99 CD**
*Our six-week  program  to optimal Health and Energy!* by  Ted and Sharon Broer

**CD 1:** The Top Ten Foods Never to Eat
**CD 2:** Forever Slim (Do's and Don'ts of Weight Loss)
**CD 3:** Winning Choices for Your Health
**CD 4:** Double Your Energy, Double Your Output
**CD 5:** Simplifying the Supermarket Safari
**CD 6:** Foods That Heal
**CD 7:** Food Choices: Facts & Myths
**CD 8:** Answers to Our Most FAQs

> Plus reports on:
> A.D.D, Hypertension, Cancer, Diabetes, Depression, and Prostate Problems

## *Maximum Energy Book $19.95*

By Ted Broer
The Top Ten Foods Never to Eat!
The Top Ten Health Strategies, for Maximum Energy.  Double your energy in 30 days with the right choices in this insightful book!

## *The Maximum Energy Cookbook  $22.99*

By Sharon Broer with Ted Broer
Over 500 recipes in this 175-page cookbook.  Maximize your energy and feel great in 6 short weeks.  With chapters on breakfast, simplifying the supermarket, children's and holiday recipes.

## *Healthy Country Cooking $24.99  BOOK*

By Sharon Broer
Grandma's Secret Recipes, The newest cookbook by Ted and Sharon Broer.
Recipes with NO: Hydrogenated Oils, Trans Fats, Nitrites, Canola Oil, Aspartame, Artificial Ingredients, Soy products

### Forever Fit: At 20, 30, 40, and Beyond $119.99 CD

Lose Weight* Feel Great* Fitness/Health Series
*Our up-to-date series on Health, Nutrition, Sports Medicine, and exercise!*

**CD 1:** Fat Loss, Not Weight Loss—The Key to Looking Great! Hormones and How They Control the body
**CD 2:** Exercise—Its Role In Burning Fat, Lean Muscle Mass—What Types & How much
**CD3:** Trace Minerals, Vitamin Supplements, Fatty Acids/ Joint Repair and Arthritis
**CD 4:** Artificial Sweeteners, Chemicals and Foods in Our Environment to Avoid
**CD 5:** Chronic Fatigue Syndrome, Yeast Infection, Hypoglycemia, and Your Immune System
**CD 6:** Constipation, the Colon, and Your Health
**CD 7:** Fasting: The Physical & Spiritual Benefits
**CD 8:** Water: Use a Filter or Be a Filter, Why You Absorb As Many Toxins in One Hot Shower As if you had drunk 8 glasses of contaminated water.

### Maximum Energy Health & Fitness $119.99 CD

Learn how to feel twenty years younger, increase your energy levels, and greatly improve your general health in just 30 days!!!

**CD 1:** What is Happening to the Health of our Country, The Wisdom of the Ages, Dead Cooked Parasites
**CD 2:** Many Medical Professionals Have No Nutritional Training, The Destruction of Our Food Supply, Top Ted Foods Not to Eat
**CD 3:** Shower Filter, Use a Filter or Be a Filter, How to Increase Libido in Men, Fake Fat
**CD 4:** Homocystine Theory of Heart Disease, Toxic Personal Care Products
**CD 5:** Cardiovascular Health, Diabetes, and Stress Management
**CD 6:** Getting Started, Trace Minerals, and Hair Analysis
**CD 7:** Warning! Contains Poison, Read the Label
**CD 8:** How to Easily Break Food Addictions
**Plus** reports on Attention Deficit Disorder, Depression, Hypertension, Diabetes, Prostate/Impotency/Infertility, Maintaining Muscle Mass and Losing Body Fat, Chronic Fatigue Syndrome, and Hemorrhoids & Constipation

### Eat, Drink and Be Healthy Exercise DVD's $79.99

By Ted Broer
*A Scientific Approach to Athletic Conditioning and Proper Nutrition.*
It Includes:

- Non Impact Training
- Lean Muscle Growth & Fat Loss in 6 Weeks
- For Men and Women of all ages
- Three tape series for Men or Women - 6 total tapes
- Lifetime warranty on videos

## Understanding God's Dietary Principles $27.00

*This one answers all the Biblical Nutrition Questions*
By Ted Broer

**Tape 1:** How God's Dietary Principles Relate to Us
**Tape 2**: In Depth Scriptural Overview
**Tape 3**: How to Break the Dietary Curses of Degenerative Disease

## Hypoglycemia: A Sensible Approach $27.00

By Ted Broer

**Tape 1:** Sugar & Controlling Hypoglycemia
**Tape 2:** Sugar & the American Sweet Tooth
**Tape 3:** What has Happened to Our Health? *If you have it, you need this series.*

## Breaking the Dietary Curses of Cancer  $39.00

By Ted Broer

**Tape 1:** Cancer Prevention
**Tape 2:** The Benefits of Fasting
**Tape 3:** Fiber and a Healthy Colon
**Tape 4:** God's Dietary Principles
**Tape 5:** Clean & Unclean Foods
*The nation's 2nd largest killer can be prevented.*

## Nutrition and Your Healthy Heart $27.00

By Ted Broer

**Tape 1:** Preventing Heart Disease
**Tape 2:** Exercising the Smart Way
**Tape 3:** Stress and Your Health
*Learn how to keep this critical organ in top shape.*

## Helping Your Family Make Dietary Changes $27.00

By Ted & Sharon Broer

**Tape 1:** Fiber & Food Preparation
**Tape 2:** Healthy Food Substitutes
**Tape 3:** Attitudes on Nutrition
*This one makes it easy!*

### Preventing Arthritis and Osteoporosis $27.00
By Ted Broer

**Tape 1:** Arthritis and Osteoporosis
**Tape 2:** The Importance of Calcium
**Tape 3:** Is Supplementation Necessary?
*It's easier to prevent!*


### Train Up A Child In the Way He Should Eat $27.00
By Sharon Broer

**Tape 1:** Prenatal Nutrition
**Tape 2:** Infant & Toddler Nutrition
**Tape 3:** A Child's Diet, a *must for those with children.*


### *Natural Cooking for the Holidays $21.00*
By Sharon Broer

**Tape 1:** Using Meat Replacements and Grains
**Tape 2:** Holiday Meal Planning
**Tape 3:** Sugar Replacements and Holiday Desserts
*For those who ask, "Where do I start?"*


### Maximum Fat Loss Book   $24.99
By Ted Broer

- The alarming truth about protein diets.
- The twelve-step program to lose body fat, not muscle.
- What weight loss products you should never use.
- 3 easy steps to stop the obese child epidemic.
- The key to permanently speeding up your metabolism.
- Discover 5 secret supplements that melt body fat and cellulite.
- Why you should never drink diet sodas.


### Maximum Fat Loss Workbook $19.99
*By Ted Broer*

- *Learn how to make a commitment rooted in desire.*
- *Set realistic goals and motivating rewards.*
- *Set the right calorie count and divide it over multiple meals.*
- *Learn the right types and amounts of protein to eat at every meal.*
- *Add the right kinds and amount of carbohydrates at every meal.*

- *Drink the right type of beverage ever day.*
- *Take sufficient fiber every day.*
- *Eat "essential" fats at every meal.*
- *Exercise several times a week.*
- Take the best supplements daily to help your body fight fat.

### *Maximum Memory By Ted Broer $24.99  BOOK*

- *The 10 most powerful nutrients to enhance memory.*
- *Alzheimer's therapies that really work.*
- *How to boost test scores.*
- *Stroke prevention and recovery.*
- *Key memory building exercises.*
- *4 key strategies for stopping Senile Dementia.*
- *3 products that actually poison the brain.*
- *"Smart" foods and herbs.*

### *Maximum Age Reversal $34.99 BOOK*
*By Ted Broer*

- *Staying heart disease and cancer free*
- *Which supplements really work to reverse the aging process?*
- *10 Key secrets to looking and feeling 20 years younger*
- *Stress free living made simple*
- *Hormone replacement therapy*
- *Cutting edge age reversal therapies*

### *Maximum Solutions for ADD, Learning Disabilities, and Autism  $24.99*
*By Ted Broer*

- *Top 5 foods never to feed a hyperactive child*
- *Truth about measles, immunizations and autism*
- *Natural treatments for A.D.D. A.D.H.D. and Autism*

### *Maximum Success CD's $119.99*
### *By Ted Broer*

- *Healthy choices for maximum energy and vitality, living the balanced life*
- *Top 35 reasons why you're not prospering*
- *34 Key leadership strategies to becoming super successful*
- *Personal development—becoming all you were meant to be*

199

- *Stress management—how to stop worrying and start living*
- *28 secrets of starting a successful business with little or no money*

**Bonus CD's:**
*Trace mineral supplementation*

*Toxic personal care products and how to find*
*if you have vitamin and mineral*
*deficiencies.*

# *GREAT NUTRITION PRODUCTS*

**Suggested by Ted Broer**
To Order, call 1-800-726-1834, www.healthmasters.com
**All Prices Subject to Change**

**Adrenal Support $25.99**
Supports stress response and adrenal hormone production. 60 caps

**Ag-Cidal Colloidal Silver        $52.00**
Natural antibiotic, great for infections, bacteria cannot live in its presence.

**All-One** Powder multiple vitamin and mineral supplement. Tastes great in a smoothie, excellent energy booster
**15.9 oz.............$32.95**
**2.2 lb...............$55.95**

**Aloe Vera Juice $7.95**
Excellent for constipation. Use as a laxative and/or digestive aid. 32 oz.

**Alpha Lipoic Acid $17.50**
A powerful antioxidant, helps to rebuild cells and eliminate toxins. 60 caps

**AquaTrace        $21.00**
80 colloidal minerals in a liquid suspension. 100% absorbable  32 oz.

**Ascorbate C Powder $24.00**
Ph neutral vitamin C powder, strengthens immune system and prevents cancer, fights infection.  8 oz.

**Atri Aloe        $19.95**
Natural aloe laxative, keeps the system cleansed.  100 capsules

**Barley Grass        $18.00**
Natural wheat grass supplement, great for trace minerals.  100 caps

**Beet Juice Tablets**
**$23.95**
Organically grown beets, great source for trace minerals, aids in rejuvenating red blood cells  150 tabs

**Blackstrap Molasses**
**$4.50    15 oz.**
A great source of all natural iron for children and adults with anemia.

**Black Walnut Tincture**
**$34.95**
Kills parasites within the body.  4 oz.

**Borage Oil        $29.99**
Omega fatty acid complex, great for skin, hair, nails & joints. 90 ct

**Cal-Apatite    $19.95**
Chewable calcium supplement.  Children will love the great chocolate flavor.  90 tabs

**Carnitine        $27.99**
All natural L-Carnitine, amino acid, great fat burner.  60 caps

**Chelation Therapy**
**$29.95      120 capsules**
Oral chelation, removes heavy metals.

**Childrens DHA  $25.99**
Childrens omega fatty acid, promotes brain and visual development, great strawberry flavor 180 chewable gels

**Children's Cod Liver Oil    $26.99**
100% arctic cod liver oil, supports memory, learning and visual development, great strawberry flavor. 8 oz.

**Cholesterol-X    $24.98**
Raises good cholesterol, lowers bad cholesterol and triglyceride levels.

**Chondro Relief  $34.98**
Joint and bone support, rebuilds cartilage, reduces joint swelling, excellent product for arthritis. 120 caps

**Cinnamon Extract Fuel Burner        $39.99**
Therapeutic blend to support insulin

sensitivity, and promote healthy blood sugar levels; for those with diabetes, hypertension due to high body fat levels and insulin resistance.  120 caps

**Cloves          $6.50**
Aids in killing parasites within the body. 100 ct

**Cod Liver Oil**
Natural Omega-3 fatty acid, helps strengthen immune system, lowers cholesterol and acts as a natural anti-inflammatory.
**250  capsules…..$12.95**
**liquid  16 oz …...$16.00**

**Coenzyme Q 10  $48.00**
A must for proper heart function and circulation, lowers blood pressure, great antioxidant. 60 ct.

**Cortico B**
**120 caps     $31.99**
**240 caps     $44.99**
Supports the adrenal system, regulates the body energy production, great for allergies and asthma.  120 capsules

**Detoxificant     $18.00**
Natural detoxificant, contains bentonite which has been used for centuries for its healing properties  32 oz.

**DHEA               $19.95**
Anti aging and energy, "The Mother of All Hormones" helps you look and feel younger!

**Digestive Enzyme**
**$47.00**
Contains plant enzyme fortifiers, a must for digestive problems. 270

**Digestive Enzyme**
**Blend            $24.00**
Digestive aid, also great for heartburn.  90 caps

**Dimension        $34.95**
Management of estrogen dominant conditions, helpful for those with endometriosis, polycystic ovarian syndrome, fibrocystic breasts, menstrual irregularities, endometriosis and uterine fibroids.  120 ct

**DMAE Eye Cream $17.99**
Firms the sagging skin under the eyes.

**DMAE Lotion $25.00**
Revitalizing lotion with alpha lipoic acid and vitamin c ester.

**Echinacea $10.49**
Great immune system support 100 caps

**Eliminator Mouthwash $9.99**
All natural mouthwash promotes healthy teeth and a healthy mouth.

**Enhanced Sleep Support $33.50**
Normalizes nighttime stress hormones and enhances sleep; reduces stress and anxiety. 60 ct

**Ester-C Powder $29.95**
Unique form of vitamin C containing naturally occurring metabolites, gentle on digestive system, strengthens immune system. 8 oz

**Estro Cream $23.99**
Support for female reproductive tissues, normalizes estrogen levels. 2 oz.

**Evening Primrose Oil $12.99**
Great for the skin, wrinkle reduction, eczema, psoriasis, and healthy hormone balance. 60 caps

**Excellent C $29.99**
Great for the immune system, best C on the market. 120 caps

**Eyesight $49.99**
Excellent for the support and care of the eyes, maintains healthy retina, lens and eyesight function. 60 caps

**Fat Burner CLA-1 $39.99**
Conjugated Linoleic Acid, great fat burner and cellulite reducer, turns fat into lean muscle. 120 softgels

**Feminine Rinse  $13.20**
Liquid concentrate, great for candida and yeast infections.  4 oz

**Folic Acid          $8.50**
A must to take before pregnancy to prevent birth defects. 100 caps

**Flax Seed Oil**
Natural organic Omega-3 fatty acid, great for the skin and helps to lower cholesterol.
**180 caps          $23.00**
**16 oz liquid     $19.99**

**Garlic            $20.00**
Excellent for yeast infections, immune system, and aids in eliminating toxins within the body.  90 caps

**Gastragest      $17.50**
Nutritional support for a well functioning digestive system, excellent for belching and gas.  90 capsules

**Get Lean Protein $39.99**
Weight loss meal, reduces the risk of cancer. Comes in chocolate or vanilla.  14 servings

**GHI Cleanse        $58.00**
Supplies optimal cleansing nutrition for those with conditions associated with gastrointestinal, hepatic or inflammatory disorders.  14 servings

**Glucomannan     $15.49**
Great source of vegetable fiber, helps in fat reduction . 100 caps

**Glutamine        $37.99**
Support for the integrity and optimal function of the intestinal lining. 30

**Grayslake Gelatin. $16.00**
Great product for joint pain and arthritis, also strengthens hair and nails.  16 oz

**Greenlife Tablets $49.95**
All natural food concentrate, a great source of minerals and enzymes.  360 tabs

**GSE Capsules    $14.00**
Grapefruit seed extract
in a soft gel, equivalent
to 12-15 drops of the
liquid concentrate. 90ct

**GSE  Liquid
Concentrate    $11.95**
Amazing multi-purpose
formula, excellent for
sore throats, stomach
irritation, skin and scalp
conditions.  Also makes
a wonderful fruit and
vegetable wash. 2 oz.

**Hair Factors      $31.95**
Provides minerals and
nutrients necessary for
hair growth.  100 tabs

**Healthy Lipid Profile
$36.00**
Lowers cholesterol with
antioxidant citrus bio-
flavonoids, reduces
inflammation  60 caps

**HGH Stimulate  $79.95**
Improves memory,
lowers body fat and
reduces cellulite, reduces
wrinkles, increases bone
density, exercise
performance, energy and
erectile function 60 serv.

**Hydroxycitrate Plus
$33.99          90 tablets**
Blocks the conversion of
carbohydrates to fat.
Incredible product!

**Immune Support
$33.99          120 caps**
High potency
immunoglobulin
concentrate, protects the
immune system

**Insulin Support $24.95**
Herbal and nutrient
support for healthy
blood sugar, provides
support for glucose and
insulin metabolism. 60ct

**Intestinal Cleanser
$16.00**
Aids in removing debris
accumulated in the
colon.  10 oz.

**L-Arginine      $14.50**
Free form amino acid,
great fat loss product

**L-Lysine         $9.95**
Free form amino acid,
great fat loss product

**L-Ornithine    $25.00**
Free form amino acid, great fat loss product.

**Lecithin          $12.95**
Protects against cardiovascular disease, promotes energy, helps lower cholesterol, great for memory. 16 oz

**Liver Support    $21.99**
Supports healthy liver function and aid in protection of liver tissue.

**Magnesium and Malate Acid          $23.00**
Magnesium supplement for a healthy heart 120 caps

**Menopause Support $25.00        120 caps**
Targeted nutritional support for women during menopause.

**Melatonin      $11.99**
Natural product of the pineal gland, lets you sleep like a baby.

**Memory Support $39.99        60 Caps**
Nutrient and botanical blend, for optimum cognitive function, and memory enhancement.

**Milk Thistle        $20.00**
Cleanses and purifies the liver. 60 caps

**Mitochondrial Resuscitate      $52.95**
Nutritional support for healthy cellular energy production. 60 tabs

**Mood Formula $27.99**
Nervous system support, promotes a healthy mood. 60 caps

**Multigenics Chewable $19.95          90 count**
Foundation nutrition for children and adults. Great orange flavor.

**Multigenics Powder $23.00    18 servings**
Powdered multi-vitamin supplement.

**Multi-Prenatal   $36.95**
Excellent for pregnant and nursing mothers.

**Mycelized Children's Multi**    **$17.99**
Foundational nutrition for infants and toddlers.

**Mycelized Vitamin A $19.95**
Great for the skin and immune system.

**N-Acetyl Cysteine $15.99**    **60 caps**
Supports detoxification of environmental toxins and heavy metals, healthy respiratory function, powerful antioxidant.

**Nail Rescue**    **$9.96**
Protects nails from the discomfort of nail fungus, also strengthens weak and brittle nails.

**Nasal Spray**    **$14.99**
Natural, non-irritating nasal spray, contains colloidal silver, perfect for colds, allergies and sinus infections. 1 oz

**Norwegian Omega 3 $37.99**    **120 caps**
Essential fatty acids from cold water fish

**Ossomag**    **$29.50**
Excellent calcium supplement for strong bones and teeth, also contains magnesium and vitamin D.    120 caps

**Ouch & Itch Spray $7.80**
A must for every medicine cabinet! Use on wounds, cuts, scrapes, poison ivy, after shaving, even as a deodorant. 4 oz.

**PhosphaLine**    **$68.50**
Excellent for cirrhosis, hepatitis C, memory loss, gallstones, and psoriasis. 100 softgels

**PMS Support**    **$38.50**
Nutritional support for women with symptoms associated with menstrual cycles. 120 ct

**Power of 3**    **$16.74**
Immune system support, protects against infections. 90 caps

**Probiotic Blend  $27.99**
Yeast infection, natural bowel function, lactose intolerance  84 caps

**Progesterone Cream $39.95**
Natural progesterone cream eases the symptoms of PMS and helps with mood swings, abdominal cramps, and water retention.

**Prostality        $37.00**
Great supplement for male health, impotency and prostate function. 60 soft gels

**Pycnogenol    $50.00**
Standardized pine bark extract.  The most powerful antioxidant on the market today.60 caps
**Salicin          $23.00**
All natural pain reliever and anti-inflammatory.

**Saw Palmetto   $17.95**
Helps to maintain a healthy prostate.  100 ct

**Serenex          $35.99**
Chinese herbal stress remedy, promotes a

sense of inner calm and helps you rest better.120

**Soothing Ear Drops $7.20**
Great for children and adults alike, offers soothing relief, quickly and gently.  1 oz.

**Sublingual B-12  $33.90**
Great tasting sublingual B-12, great for energy.

**Super Potent E   $16.00**
Excellent for heart, circulation, and cancer prevention.  60 soft gels

**Throat Relief Spray $7.80**
Great for dry, scratchy and raw throats, also works well as a breath spray, available in cherry and wintergreen. 1 oz.

**Thyroid Support $29.99**
Supports healthy thyroid hormone levels. 120 ct

**Tom's of Maine Toothpaste        $6.39**
All natural, fluoride free toothpaste, cinnamon

**Tom's of Maine Deodorant    $6.39**
All natural aluminum free deodorant. Available in unscented, rose and wood-spice

**Toxi-Cleanse Plus $59.90   21 servings**
Supplies optimal cleansing nutrition for those with conditions associated with toxicity.

**Traveler's Friend $3.98**
Add to drinking water to purify, great to use when traveling.

**Tribulus Fuel    $18.95**
Helps to elevate testosterone levels 100 ct

**Triple Yeast Defense $16.74**
Amazing formula for candida and yeast infections.  90 caps

**Ultimate Essentials $44.99**
Daily dose-pack nutrition, each pack contains (2) Ultimate Multiple, (1)

Antioxidant Support and (1) Norwegian Omega 3…provides convenient and comprehensive nutritional support.  60 packet (1 month supply)

**Ultimate Essentials Women $57.99**
Daily dose-pack nutrition, each pack contains (2) Ultimate Multiple, (1) Antioxidant Support and (1) Norwegian Omega 3 and (2 Ossomag provides convenient nutritional support.  60 packet (1 month supply)

**Ultimate Immune Booster    $31.90**
Powerful antioxidant and detoxifier, protects against all types of cancer    30 caps

**Ultimate Multiple $23.99    120 caps**
Multi-vitamin and mineral complex

**Ultra Potent C Chewable $19.95**

Great for children's vitamin C needs, has a pleasant tasting.  90 tabs

## Ultra Shine Toothpaste $9.99
All natural, fluoride free toothpaste freshens breath and gives your teeth a sparkling shine!

## Urinary Tract Support $34.95
All natural support for a healthy urinary tract, contains d-mannose, a simple sugar found in pineapples and cranberries  50 servings

## Vascular Relaxant $26.50   120 caps
Sustained release niacin, great for high blood pressure and cardiovascular health

## Vaso B6          $15.00
Natural muscle relaxant, great for PMS  100 tabs

## Virility          $29.99
Male sexual enhancer, supports healthy sexual function. 60 soft gels

## Whey Protein     $40.50
Lactose free, low in fat and carbs, complete amino acid profile. 2 lbs. Vanilla or chocolate flavor.

## Wormwood          $9.99
Kills parasites within the body  100 caps

## Wrinkle Relief Cream$25.98  2 OZ.
Helps nourish your skin and rebuilds collagen.

## Zinc Glycinate    $19.90
For immune support, healthy tissue and prostate health.  120 caps